Congratulations!
It's a Dog!

Training and Behavior Tips for the
Newest Member of Your Family

D. Caroline Coile, Ph.D.

BARRON'S

Acknowledgment

The author is greatly indebted to Lynne Daurelle, Ph.D,
for her valuable contributions to the text—as
well as comic relief during writing!

Illustrations by Tom Kerr

All inquiries should be addressed to:
Barron's Educational Series, Inc.
250 Wireless Boulevard
Hauppauge, NY 11788
www.barronseduc.com

ISBN-13: 978-0-7641-3123-3
ISBN-10: 0-7641-3123-0

Library of Congress Catalog Card No. 2005041078

Library of Congress Cataloging-in-Publication Data
    Coile, D. Caroline.
        Congratulations! It's a dog! : training and behavior tips for the
    newest member of your family / Caroline Coile.
        p. cm
        ISBN 0-7641-3123-0
        Dogs—Miscellanea. 2. Dogs—Training—Miscellanea. I. Title.

    SF426.2.C6455 2005
    636.7—dc22   2005041078

Printed in the United States of America
9 8 7 6 5 4 3 2 1

Contents

Preface

Congratulations! You're taking the first steps to enjoying a fulfilling life with your dog!

Dogs are true members of the family, loved as you would any other important member, but nonetheless very different in their needs and abilities. Only by understanding your dog's behavior can you effectively mold that behavior. Presented here are the latest scientific findings to show you how to raise your dog with love, logic, and liver, guiding you on your way to sharing a fulfilling and harmonious life with your canine family member.

- Do you want to know why dogs do what they do? Start with Chapter 1, and discover what dogs are—and aren't. You'll see how they are neither furkids nor house-wolves, and how their evolution shaped their current behavior and relationships with people.

- Do you want to know how to find the best match for you? Check out Chapter 2 to learn breed propensities for behavior, and how trainability, aggression, and friendliness are inherited. Find out how early experiences affect your puppy's adult behavior, and how that affects where you should get your dog.

- Do you want to know how to communicate with your dog? Read Chapter 3 to find out how dogs and people commonly misunderstand each other. Learn how you can communicate using visual, auditory, tactile, and olfactory cues.

- Do you want to know how to be fair without being overly permissive? Then you need Chapter 4, where you will learn about current thinking regarding house rules, bed sleeping, crate time, and overall good behavior.

- Do you want to know how to raise a well adjusted dog? Chapter 5 explains everything your dog needs to learn—and the best way to teach him—during his wonder weeks.

- Do you want to know how to save your carpets? Hurry to Chapter 6 to learn the newest methods of house training. They work!

- Do want to know how to best motivate your dog to do what you want? Chapter 7 is the first of three chapters you need to read before you start training. Learn why punishment can't compete with rewards, and learn the best ways to use rewards to get the behavior you want.

- Do you want to know how to get your dog to understand what you want? That's where Chapter 8 will help. Learn the right way to clicker train and shape behavior—and how to get rid of unwanted behavior.

- Do you want to know how to teach some specific actions? Chapter 9 gives you step-by-step recipes for getting handy household behaviors—and for getting rid of some common household misbehaviors.

- Do you want to know how to deal with behavior problems in general? Chapter 10 gives you insights, options, and hope.

- Do you want to know how to help your anxious dog? In Chapter 11 you'll learn how to handle dogs with separation anxiety, fears, and obsessive-compulsive disorders. They're more common than you think.

- Do you want to know how to handle your aggressive dog? Turn to Chapter 12 for help before things get too bad. Different types of aggression call for different treatments; did you know that most canine aggression is not your fault?

NOTE: Throughout this book, all dogs are referred to as "he" and all people as "she" unless referring to something gender-specific. There is no deep hidden meaning in this convention.

Chapter 1
Bones of Contention

Congratulations! It's a boy! It's a girl! It's a dog!

Expecting a new family member is exciting, but if you're like most new parents, it's also daunting. Even if you've raised bald human babies, this furry canine baby is going to be challenging. For one thing, he's gifted in comparison. He'll learn to walk, talk, and feed himself when he's just a few weeks old. Being the parent of a gifted child means you will need to learn everything at gifted speed. Just as with child rearing, you're going to get a lot of weird advice from people whose authority comes from the fact that they once raised a dog or a child and it never killed anybody. Given the quality of some of their advice, that achievement is often amazing.

Furkids? The first thing you'll encounter is the argument about how you should be thinking about your dog. Is he really a family member? Most people in our society do consider their dogs to be real members of the family. But that doesn't necessarily mean we should consider them our "furbabies" or "furkids," as some people do. Dogs do share many traits with children, we often love them as we do our children, and we can use many child-rearing principles with them, but thinking of dogs as children in fur suits does both dogs and children a disservice.

House-wolves? Other dog owners think of their dogs as wolves that have moved into their homes. Their owners are not their dog's parents, but their pack leaders. This, too, does the dog a disservice.

Dogs are not furry kids, nor are they housebound wolves. They are dogs, glorious dogs, and that's their mystique and their challenge.

It's a Dog's Life

How should we think of this species that is so much a part of our lives? Dogs have been worshipped, vilified, eaten, pampered, and ignored in various cultures throughout history. Even in our society, where we spend billions of dollars each year on pet luxuries, many dogs are still misunderstood, neglected, abused, and abandoned.

We think our dogs are the luckiest dogs there have ever been, and in some senses, they are. They get the best food and health care of any dogs in history. They have laser light toys and microchip identification. But maybe they're not so lucky. We have latchkey dogs who spend hours alone. Unemployment has hit crisis proportions as working dogs sit idle. We have dogs who are in retirement homes before they are even grown. The one thing our dogs really want the most is what we have so little of: our time.

It's a job! Dogs have been employed as hunters, draft animals, guardians, and herders, but today their major job is as companion. It's not a new job; the Egyptians had lapdogs at least by the fifth century B.C. Nor is our sentimental attachment to dogs anything new. An ancient Greek tombstone marking a dog's grave reads:

"...Laugh not, I pray thee,
Though it is a dog's grave, tears fell for me,
And the dust was heaped above me by a master's hand,
Who likewise engraved these words upon my tomb."

Our attachments to dogs grow from our interactions with them. In societies in which dogs are just strays, people may feed them but they don't form relationships with them. Only when dogs begin to work cooperatively with people do relationships tend to form. Dogs that do something noteworthy are objects of pride and claims of ownership. In our society, dogs that are kept in pens out back have no chance to form relationships with their owners, and are often abandoned. To ensure a lasting relationship with your dog, you need to share adventures and develop a sense of pride in him. To do that, you need to teach him to be a trustworthy companion. And he can't learn that on his own.

New Tricks of the Trade

"So to bed, where my wife and I had some high words upon my telling her that
I would fling the dog which her brother gave her out the window if he pissed
the house any more."
                                        —Diary of Samuel Pepys, February 12, 1660

Later entries from Samuel Pepys' diary reveal that he did grow to love the dog, but if he cured him of "pissing the house," he didn't say how. If he used the standard advice of the time, it's probably a miracle the dog learned anything. Even the top dog book of 100 years ago, in describing housetraining, advocated

"that one thorough whipping does more good and less harm to a dog than a series of
minor corrections. He remembers it far longer, and in his heart he knows that he deserved
it for something or other, even if he has not learnt what the actual offense was."
                          —Vero Shaw, The Classic Encyclopedia of the Dog, 1879

If this makes no sense to you, then you understand learning principles far better than most dog trainers did in the past century. Punishment that the dog can't relate to his actions only serves to make the dog mistrust the offending person. Not only does it not make sense from a practical viewpoint, it's disturbing from an ethical viewpoint. Substitute the word "child" for "dog" and reread the advice. That's called child abuse. We now call it dog abuse, as well.

You can teach an old dog trainer new tricks. Dog training advice has been around since at least 320 B.C., but only recently have significant advances come on the scene. Just as with child rearing, arguments have persisted through the centuries over the relative merit of punishment versus reward. War dog training in the twentieth century relied heavily on force and punishment, and these techniques became especially popular after the wars.

Most of us don't need to ready our dogs for war, however. We can train our dogs to be trusting and trustworthy companions using less forceful techniques based on scientific learning principles. A dog training revolution has taken place recently as trainers have discovered operant and classical conditioning methods, using the same techniques that have long been used to train circus animals and performing dolphins. Many of these same methods had already come into favor for rearing children.

Save that dog! Behavior problems remain the single greatest reason that dogs are euthanized or relinquished to animal shelters. Newer understanding of canine genetics, development, communication, motivation, and training are helping owners prevent many of these problems before they become rooted. Clinical canine behaviorists, the canine counterparts of child psychiatrists, are treating established problems with behavior modification and drug therapy. Dogs are being saved.

Dogs aren't children in fur coats, but they share many development, emotional, and learning traits with children. Dogs also aren't wolves in our midst, but they share many developmental, physiological, and social aspects with them. Dogs are a unique blend of wild ancestors and dependent children. That's why we love them, and why parenting challenges arise if we raise them ignoring either part of their psyches.

It's a Child's Life

In many ways, how we view dogs reflects our changing views of children. As with dogs, children were once viewed as their parents' possessions to be used, sold, or dispensed with as their parents desired. Children who were difficult, different, or useless were disposable, so much so that foundling homes were created to house them. It does not seem reasonable that dogs should not be sold or utilized humanely, but we do hope that they will not be so easily disposed of in the future.

Children were viewed as small adults, and were considered to be purposely defiant when they did not conform to adult behaviors; they were also thought to be capable of evil thoughts and practices. Many dog owners today expect their dogs to behave in ways dogs cannot comprehend; when the dogs misbehave, their owners attribute it to motives and scheming that are beyond the dogs' mental capacity.

Child and parent education made great leaps in the twentieth century. Behavioral psychologists taught that children could be shaped as they grew, stressing the importance of early education. Now behaviorists are applying that knowledge to dogs. As a new dog parent, you will find that following their advice will help your dog become all that he can be.

A Wolf in Dog's Clothing

Although we all tend to think of our dogs as "almost human," they are not. Your dog is a dog, a card-carrying canid. He's more a wolf in sheep's clothing than he is a kid in a fur suit. More accurately, he is a wolf in a wolf pup suit. So how did this wolf go from stalking Little Red Riding Hood to begging at her table?

Cave dogs? Most of us grew up with the idea that cavemen domesticated wolves, perhaps by raising abandoned puppies. The wolf pups grew into Rin Tin Tin types, guarding the camp and helping in the hunt. By breeding Rin Tin Tin to Lassie the cavemen created domesticated dogs. The only problem with this theory is that it doesn't make sense. Why would cavemen even think to bring back cubs and go through the immense trouble of hand-raising them? Wild wolves would not have done anything to convince cavemen that they would be handy to have around the cave. Modern attempts to tame wolf pups show that you have to start with them before their eyes open, and no matter how good a job you do, once they reach sexual maturity they leave home for good. Sort of like kids, except the kids keep coming back.

Cavemen would have had a nearly impossible time confining a wolf. If you think keeping your dog in your yard is hard try containing a wolf. Yet the story goes that cavemen produced man's best friend by selecting for the tamest wolves for many generations. That would take a lot of wolves. To give you an idea of how many, a Siberian experiment begun in 1959 sought to develop domesticated foxes by rigorously selecting for tameness. After 35 generations and 75,000 foxes, they achieved a line of friendly foxes, in which about 75% actively solicited human interaction. Selection for tameness is not a short-order proposition. There's no such evidence that cavemen carried out huge wolf breeding schemes. But if early humans didn't domesticate the dog, who did?

That Domesticated Look

Why don't dogs just look and act like tame wolves? Back to those friendly foxes: a funny thing happened on the way to becoming friendly. Some of those friendly foxes developed most unfoxlike traits such as floppy ears, white coat patches, and coming into estrus twice a year—just like dogs. Somehow by selecting for tameness other traits were inadvertently also selected. Perhaps the same thing happened in our domesticated dogs. People didn't select for floppy ears or white patches; they just appeared, and never went away.

Other non-wolf traits in dogs can be explained by pressures at the dump compared to the hunting fields. Dump scavengers don't need big bodies, big teeth, or even big brains like cooperative hunters (wolves) do. These things all take energy in the form of calories to maintain, so when the pickings were slim, the smaller dump-diver with the lower caloric needs would be the survivor. Early domestic dogs probably most resembled the pariah dogs still seen wandering around the villages of some primitive cultures, depending on human waste products to survive.

Dump divers. Many canine researchers now favor the idea that dogs domesticated themselves. When humans first established villages they created waste sites, or as the wolves of the time would have called them, all-you-can-eat buffets. These smorgasbords weren't for the faint of heart; it took some brashness to dine so close to people. Those wolves that stayed and ate were at a reproductive advantage over their cautious cousins. Living was easy at the dump, and it may have also been a sort of singles bar for this tame new generation. Over many generations the tamer individuals continued to be at an advantage, some perhaps tame enough to put the dog's unsurpassed begging skills to their first test.

My, What a Small Brain You Have!

"The better to mind you with…" replies the dog. Compared to wolves, dogs are dumb. At least when it comes to wolf-smarts. Lock a dog in a pen, and he may scratch at the latch, dig, bite, bark, and finally resort to his doggy secret weapon—looking sad. Lock a wolf in a pen, and you'll have an empty pen.

One popular theory of dog domestication speculates that domestic dogs are neotenized wolves. That's a kind way of saying they are cases of arrested development. Domestic dogs are canid Peter Pans, young wolves that never grow up. Young, dumb, trusting wolves. Such a wolf would be less fearful of humans and more likely to feel at home in the dumps—or in our homes.

Compared to adult wolves, juvenile wolves have smaller brains for their size, smaller teeth, and smaller jaws. So do dogs. Compared to adult wolves, juvenile wolves are less resourceful, less fearful, and more trusting. So are dogs. Juvenile wolves do something adult wolves almost never do: They bark when they are alarmed. Sound like anybody you know?

Maybe dogs are both wolves and kids. They are the kiddie version of a wolf, perpetual wolf pups that attract us because they act in so many ways like kids. But in so many other ways, they act like dogs.

Dogs Will Be Dogs

Why do so many people get a dog and then act incredulous that he acts like a dog? Do they expect him to sit at the table and choose the right fork for his salad? Then why do they expect him to do other undoggy things? Here's a clue: Dogs act like dogs because it's in their genes. Their DNA commands them: Bark. Chew. Dig. Chase. Drive your person crazy doing things she can't understand.

Dogs bark. For juvenile wolves, barking could be a life saver. If an intruder came to the den area while the adults were away, barking alerted the adults to come home on the run. If juveniles were separated from the rest of the pack, barking or howling could help bring the other pack members to the rescue.

Barking in response to intruders was an especially valuable trait when early dogs started hanging around villages. With their keen senses they were better than any dozing sentry, and to this day dogs have prevented more thefts than the most sophisticated monitoring devices ever sold. Barking and howling may have served as auditory beacons to summon the pack, but they serve as social irritants when modern day dogs try to summon us home from work all day. Barking in excitement may also have summoned the pack, but these days it's more likely to summon the police with a complaint.

Dogs dig. Wild canids dig for several reasons. They excavate dens in which to raise young, and they bury food for later consumption. They dig out prey. Northern dogs dig to escape the cold and southern dogs dig to escape the heat. All dogs can dig to escape confinement. Young wolves practice digging as part of their play repertoire, and since domestic dogs retain so many behaviors of young wolves, they include digging as part of their day's entertainment. The problem arises when our dogs, especially those confined to our pristine yards, turn digging into a fine art.

Dogs chew. A dog's mouth is a handy all-in-one tool that grips, carries, bites, licks, rips, and chews. These are skills an adult canid will need, and so they are the skills a young wolf—or dog—will need to perfect. Unfortunately, young house dogs perfect their skills on your new shoes, antique furniture, and feather pillows.

Dogs steal. Dogs have a survival code that starts with "Fill thy belly." The early dump dogs didn't ask permission before they made off with a hunk of carrion. The first time your dog nonchalantly picks a slice of meat off your counter he has no idea you have some far-fetched rule about not helping himself. After all, another part of the code clearly states "Dog helps those who help themselves."

Dogs scavenge. How thoughtful of you to provide a miniature dumpsite right in the kitchen or outside the backdoor. How bizarre you must seem to oppose your dog's foraging in it, the very basis of the human-dog relationship. He was only trying to be a dog.

Dogs distress. Or at least, get very upset when left alone. Although there are lone wolves, the typical wolf, especially juvenile wolf, is a pack member. To be left alone is to be put in danger, and a resourceful young wolf would do everything it could to reunite with the pack, including digging, escaping, barking, and howling—or as we call it, freaking out. The behaviorists call it separation anxiety.

Dogs lick. Many people consider it endearing that their dog gives them kisses. Others consider it disgusting. After all, we know where their tongues have been. Licking is a natural dog behavior, but its origin may not be as romantic as you might like. Puppies lick one another as an appeasement gesture, often along with rolling over and giving the canine equivalent of "Uncle!" But what puppies mostly use licking for is to elicit regurgitation from adults, particularly from their dam, around the time of weaning. Wild canids greet adults returning from hunting by licking at the adults' mouths in hopes of getting a free meal. Domestic dogs continue this behavior into adulthood, licking at the mouth of their leader, whether canine or human.

Dogs sniff. Sniffing is your dog's way of checking out a visitor's I.D. card, reading the fine print, and knowing the history of who's been where. Certain parts of dogs and people give out more odors and information than others. Dogs have no idea why we get so offended when they try to sniff these information-highway areas of our bodies. After all, they don't get offended when we read their license tags.

Dogs guard. Wild canids naturally protect their resources, whether food, territory, or offspring. Guarding is such a valuable trait that the tendency to guard has been accentuated in many domesticated breeds. But this same tendency can be troublesome if the dog guards what it perceives as its personal possessions, such as food, toys, and bed, from its human family.

Dogs bite. People hunt, fight, and protect themselves with weapons. So do dogs. The dog's weapons are its teeth, and it perfects its hunting and fighting skills through play that involves play biting. This biting is often too rough for our fragile human skin and clothes, and even too rough for other pups and dogs. Puppies learn that when they play too rough, their playmate either gives them a warning rebuke or quits playing with them, so they learn to inhibit their bites. But when needed, they still have the ability to bite—some more than others.

Dogs fight. Dogs come from a culture of both cooperation and competition. A dog that exudes leadership will tend to remain unchallenged at the top of the pack and will fight less than one in the middle of the pack. Dogs may fight other dogs for leadership, to keep them out of their territory, or to keep them away from resources. Of course, not every aggressive encounter results in a full blown fight. Dogs communicate their aggressive intentions with growls, stares, rigid posturing, and direct confrontations, all of which give the other dog a chance to back down.

Dogs mount. Sure it's embarrassing when your dog humps your visitor's leg, but don't make matters worse by telling her it must be her sex appeal. Dogs mount (and hump) for several reasons, not all of which are sexual. Young canids mount one another as part of play behavior, with the sex of the mounter or mountee inconsequential. This play behavior may play a role similar to play fighting and play hunting, preparing the pup for adult behaviors.

Most adult humpers are intact (uncastrated) males. They are more likely to engage in mounting behavior in the presence of a female dog in estrus—even if they can't reach her and must settle for another dog, a human leg, or a blow-up dog. Some dogs may have received sufficient sexual gratification from these alternate sexual targets that they continue to focus on them, unencumbered by social mores.

Female dogs in estrus or pseudopregnancy will often mount other dogs, especially other females. Even castrated males may continue to mount other dogs or objects. Although they may be acting in a sexual manner, many other cases of mounting are probably asexual. More dominant males and even females are more likely to mount other dogs. If they mount a subordinate dog, the mountee tends to put up with it, but mounting a superior may elicit a strong adverse reaction!

Dogs roam. Wild canids have a territory over which they regularly hunt. It would be highly unlikely that a wild canid, or even an early domesticated dog, could sustain itself on what it caught or scavenged in an area the size of the typical suburban yard. Even a well-fed dog retains the urge to go walkabout. Unfortunately, unless you live on hundreds of acres, this means walking about roads and neighbors' yards.

Dogs chase. Wolves have long legs, strong jaws, and sharp teeth for a reason: They are hunters. They search out, stalk, chase, and kill prey. After serving as garbage disposal and burglar alarm, one of the dog's earliest services to humans was as a hunting partner. Different aspects of the hunting repertoire were selected until we now have some dogs that perform the entire stalk, chase, and kill sequence; others that show a truncated sequence of just stalk and chase; and still others that show an even more abbreviated sequence of just stalk. Those that still have chasing as part of their hunting behavior pattern will chase. They will chase wild and domestic animals, but lacking that, they may chase cars, bikes, people, and toys. Wolves not only hunt, they kill. Domestic dogs retain that capacity in greater or lesser degree, depending on breed.

Dogs roll in disgusting things. Well, there's no easy explanation for this one. It's been said they do so to rub their scent on it as a means of claiming it for their own. It seems hard to believe they would bother to rub their scent on rotted carcasses or animal dung and not bother to rub it on a favorite bone. It's also been said they do so to disguise their own scent. Yet it seems far-fetched that any prey would find what smelled like a giant advancing pile of feces unworthy of alarm. Maybe dogs roll in disgusting things just to remind us they are dogs: *"I am canine, smell me stink!"*

Baby Power

Before you run away in horror at the idea of letting such a beast into your home, consider that children are not much better—and maybe even worse. They may not bark, but they make up for it with crying, screaming, and non-stop babbling up until the time they leave home. They dig and chew; they're just not quite as talented at it as dogs! Kids innocently steal and scavenge, they get upset when left alone, they guard their belongings overzealously, they bite and fight, and they wander and explore. They may not embarrass us by sniffing company in embarrassing places, but they make up for it with embarrassing questions. Perhaps most of all, kids, like dogs, love disgusting things—especially if they can get a reaction out of adults!

Baby face. So the next time you shake your head in disbelief that you have allowed such a wild beast into your home, ask yourself first if you're thinking of your child or your dog. Why do we put up with it? Babies and puppies come equipped with behaviors and physical features that evolved to tug at our heartstrings. These tiniest and most defenseless creatures in our home rule not with an iron fist but with a baby face. Studies have shown that we, along with most other care-giving species, naturally respond in a maternal way to animals with big rounded foreheads, big eyes, and big heads overall—all traits of babies of most species. Many dogs keep such traits their entire lives, but even without them we are already helplessly hooked. People tend to treat their dogs like children because evolution has predisposed us to treat them that way—in one sense they truly are our children in fur suits.

A Lick and a Promise

Most people welcome their new puppy with great optimism. They enjoy his puppy antics, show his picture to all their friends, and brag about his accomplishments as though he were entering medical school. But many of these same people can be found a year later giving that same dog a nonchalant pat good-bye as they drop him at the animal shelter. What happened?

The top three reasons dogs are relinquished to shelters are a change in the person's lifestyle, the time factor of caring for a dog, and behavioral problems. These are mostly people problems, not dog problems.

Lifestyle changes. Lifestyle changes include such things as moving, divorcing, marrying, or having a baby. Would such changes justify getting rid of a child? Many of these changes can be predicted; don't get a dog if you think you will have a change that will prevent you from keeping him. And many of these changes, with a little effort, can accommodate your dog. Don't welcome a family member into your home unless you mean it for keeps.

Time. Time is a factor in caring for a dog. That should be no surprise. Dogs require food, housing, grooming, and veterinary care, but most of all, they require attention. They need mental and physical activity, and they need social interaction with you or with another dog. Tally up your available time before you get a dog.

Behavior problems. The greatest killer of dogs in this country is not rabies, parvovirus, or distemper. It is ignorance. It is ignorance that allows dogs to develop and maintain behavioral problems, which are in turn the main reason dogs are euthanized. It's estimated that at least eight million animals are euthanized at shelters because of behavioral problems each year. Most of these behavior problems are the result of poor training and management—again, people problems, not dog problems. Such commonly reported but preventable problems include barking, chewing, begging, house-soiling, jumping on furniture, jumping on people, running away, disobedience, overactivity, stealing food, and destructive behavior.

This is not to say that all behavior problems your dog develops are your fault, any more than all of your child's behavior problems are your fault. Dogs and children are the products of both their genes and their environments. Sometimes, even those from the best families and best homes develop problems. Don't waste time feeling guilty; find out what you can do to make things better.

Your dog is not just your "furkid" when it's convenient and cute for him to be. He depends on you, and you need to do your part and learn to be the best parent you can be to make him the best dog he can be.

"His name is not wild dog anymore, but the first friend, because he will be our friend for always and always and always."

—Rudyard Kipling (1865–1936)

Chapter 2
Body and Soul

Congratulations! You're adopting!

Whether you already have a dog, you're getting a new dog, or you're still trying to choose a new dog, knowing about inborn predispositions can help you understand what makes your dog tick.

If you're still trying to choose, you're one of the smart ones. Unlike having a child, where it can be a little touchy to bypass your spouse in search of better baby-making material, it's perfectly acceptable and even recommended that you carefully select your new dog based on his breed and parents rather than convenience.

More than skin deep. Most of us start with looks, whether we're choosing a dog or a mate. But as anyone knows who has dated a handsome jerk, looks aren't everything. Sure, it's fun to strut around town with a guy or a dog that turns heads, but you have to live with him every day! Even the ugliest dog will look beautiful once you fall in love.

You can't pick the perfect puppy from a catalog any more than you can pick the perfect baby. But you can hedge your bet by knowing what your prospective pup's ancestors were selected to do. Even if you already have a dog, understanding his genetic heritage will help you understand his behavioral quirks and maybe give you some insights into working with him.

A wolf at your side. Remember that your dog, while not a wolf, is a wolf descendent. He is the product of generations of selection that in some cases accentuated and in others diminished basic wolf behaviors. More than physical traits, behavioral traits have been the main selection criteria through the ages. It's natural that dogs bred to do different tasks tend to act in different ways.

Only in the last century have people had the option of adorning their suburban homes with breeds originating from all over the world for purposes ranging from living heating pads to dog fighting. Humans asked a lot of the wolf when we asked it to move to our human villages and work by our sides. Now we may be asking even more of the domestic dog when we ask it to come indoors from its job and sit by our sides.

Personality Profiling

The American Kennel Club, among others, assigns breeds to different groups according to their function, and these classifications provide a fairly good basis for categorizing breed behavioral tendencies. However, to make exact predictions about an individual dog based on breed alone is only slightly more accurate than doing so based on zodiac signs. These are tendencies, not absolutes.

Sporting breeds were developed to work with hunters to locate, flush, or retrieve fowl. Pointing breeds, including setters, locate birds by ranging far afield, running back and forth scenting for game, sometimes for hours. If your pointing dog seems overactive, it's because he's the perfect activity level for his job—which is not to just hang around your house. Some of the versatile pointing breeds can also hunt small mammals, and may not be great with cats. Like pointers, spaniels also search for game, but usually over a smaller area. They, and especially retrievers, bring back downed game. Don't get a retriever unless you like being awakened by the thud of a slimy tennis ball on your chest and an expectant look gazing into your eyes. The problem with sporting dogs is that everybody thinks of themselves as sporty, so they think they need a sporting dog to complete the look. While they are driving around town in their sports car wearing their sports jacket and thinking sporty thoughts, their genuine sporting dog is home ricocheting off the walls with boredom.

Hound breeds were developed to pursue mammals, doing so without human direction. Scent hounds follow an odor trail, often baying so that the hunter can follow. If you don't want a dog that will follow its nose wherever it leads, oblivious to your calls, or one that is proud of a melodious baying bark, then don't get a scenthound. Sighthounds are the Greyhound family of dogs that chase by sight, running down swift quarry and often killing it without human help. A sighthound that looked to its owner for direction or quit when he thought he was getting too far away would be a failure as a hunter. If you can't stand the thought of your dog chasing and killing a bunny, or just running to the horizon, then a sighthound isn't for you. On the other hand, sighthounds conserve their energy for these sprints. Why do you think the Greyhound's nickname is the 40-mile-per-hour couch potato?

Working breeds were developed to aid humans with their toughness and strength. Guardian breeds naturally protect people and property. They have to be courageous and even suspicious, yet biddable, to be good guards. Don't get a guardian if you don't want him to guard—even if that means guarding against your visitors. Draft breeds like to pull. Your husky pulls for a reason! Long distance draft breeds were developed to travel many miles; don't get one and think it will be satisfied with a walk around the block. Water rescue breeds were developed to be attentive and come to the aid of a person in need. They may try to save you from drowning when you're just trying to relax in the pool!

Terrier breeds were developed to be tenacious and tough. The ratters specialize in dispatching rodents around the home and fields. The go-to-ground terriers follow small, tough mammals deep into their underground lairs, confronting them and sometimes pulling them out or killing them. Like the hounds, these vermin catchers act on their own rather than waiting for human directions. They enjoy exploring underground and are gifted diggers. When hunting with a dog underground, it's important for that dog to bark vigorously so the hunter knows where the dog is and what he's doing. Facing a tough opponent requires more than a little bravado, and these characters can be bossy with their people and scrappy around other dogs. If you can't stand a dog with an attitude, or one that is a gifted barker, most vermin-catching terriers are not for you. The bull-and-terrier breeds were developed by crossing bull-baiting dogs with tenacious terriers in order to produce tough fighting dogs. It worked. Although pussycats with people, they can be bears with other dogs. Don't get a bull-and-terrier type if you aim to frequent dog parks or plan on your dog being a canine social butterfly.

Toy breeds are often miniaturized versions of big breeds. To understand their behavioral propensities you need to understand their roots. Toy spaniels like to explore, toy sighthounds like to chase, and toy terriers can be feisty. Many of the toy breeds have been developed to be lapdogs and companions, though, and may not be as inclined to hunt, pull, and chase as their ancestors. But they are still dogs, not toys.

Non-sporting breeds are another mixed bag of dogs from various backgrounds. They include guardians, bull-baiters, bird dogs, coach dogs, barkers, and companions, among others. Know the original purpose before deciding it's the breed for you.

Herding breeds were developed to control sheep and cattle. Some breeds control by staring and stalking. This behavior tends to be used with other animals as well, which can be unsettling to other dogs. Others control by barking, and they tend to bark whenever even slightly excited about anything. Some breeds control by heel nipping, and they may chase and nip at the heels of humans, especially children at play. Some breeds control by constantly patrolling an invisible boundary, working as a sort of moving fence. If pacing about makes you nervous, they are not for you. Most of the herding breeds are very active, but they also must be responsive to human commands. They need an active job or they'll be labeled hyperactive.

Mixed breeds are another mixed bag. If you know what's behind a particular mix, you can better predict its behavior. In the case of the

Labradoodle (part Labrador Retriever, part Poodle), both parents are originally retrieving bird dogs. Get your throwing arm in shape! A Lurcher (part sighthound) will tend to chase. A predominantly hound mix will tend to hunt. A Heinz 57 may be more like the earlier domesticated dogs, and may tend to be a skilled scavenger—or perhaps have hidden talents awaiting discovery.

Mutts may be homogenized blends of generations of mixes. Other mutts may instead descend directly from the first domesticated dogs without a drop of purebred blood. Such dogs may have given rise to the pariah dogs of India or the similar dogs seen in almost every country, forged by generations of fending for themselves and living by their wits. Perhaps they are, in a sense, the very purest breed of all.

Family matters. Our dogs are products of nature and nurture. A dog's breed provides a limited set of genes from which to make new members; a dog's family narrows this gene pool even further. This is why meeting your prospective dog's canine family is so important. Their personalities are the best clues about your dog's potential personality.

If you have a particular role for your dog in mind, such as a hunting partner, herding dog, or obedience competitor, finding a puppy with relatives that are successful in those fields is your best bet. But beware that a dog may be good in one field, especially a working field, but may not be an ideal companion. Many top working dogs are too overactive to be calm pets in most households. Choose your dog for the role he will really play, not for the role you fantasize for him—or for you.

Are They Hard to Train?

One of the first questions people have about a potential breed is "Are they hard to train?" In a popular survey of obedience trial judges, breeds ranked as most obedient came mostly from herding or retrieving backgrounds, jobs for which the ability to follow human cues is important. Of the breeds ranked least obedient, most were either hunting hounds (breeds in which independent thinking is critical to success), or progenitor breeds (those breeds whose DNA is most like that of ancestral wolves). The latter may be less affected by long-time selection for trainability.

Domestication is selected for dogs that have an aptitude for training. A typical wolf, which is notoriously hard to train, will react to forceful obedience training by fleeing and struggling, reactions adaptive to its life in the wild but not to human society.

Intelligence. People with highly trainable dogs will tell you that trainability and intelligence go hand in hand. People with less easily trained dogs will tell you that refusal to follow rote commands is a sign of intelligence. Both are correct. If intelligence is defined as an innate ability to perform the task for which a dog is bred, then intelligence in one breed should be defined differently from that in another. An intelligent Border Collie reads and controls sheep; an intelligent Greyhound reads and catches jackrabbits. If they switched jobs (or brains) they would both be labeled dumb.

Dogs have been used as models in genetic studies of behavior because their distinct breeds make them perfect for studying the influence of heredity on many traits, including behavior. Among the most influential of these studies were Scott and Fuller's project comparing Shetland Sheepdogs (one of the top ranked obedience breeds), Basenjis (one of the bottom ranked obedience breeds), Beagles, Wire Fox Terriers, and Cocker Spaniels, on a number of learning and social tasks. Although the dogs did respond to various tasks with different degrees of ease, the interesting finding was that no one breed excelled at every task, and different breeds tended to fail for different reasons:

- During leash training, Basenjis vigorously fought the leash, Shelties repeatedly leapt on and tripped their handlers, and Beagles howled.

- In a test of how well they could learn to remain still when being weighed, 70% of the Cocker Spaniels but only 10% of the Fox Terriers could remain still for one minute.

- In general, for tests involving forced restraint, Cocker Spaniels did best, followed by Shelties. Fox Terriers tended to play-fight when restrained by hand, but did better from a distance. Beagles seemed restless when restrained, and Basenjis attempted to escape.

The tables turned when training went from force methods to reward methods:

- When breeds were compared on their ability to run to a box containing a reward, the Basenjis were the clear stars, with Shelties lagging far behind.

- The Basenjis and Cocker Spaniels outshined the others when it came to traversing a raised plank to get to food; the Shelties mostly failed the exercise.

- The Basenjis were also best at a task that required them to use their paws to uncover a dish of food; Cocker Spaniels were worst at this task.

- The Shelties were the worst maze runners. When placed in the maze they tended to become upset and hesitant compared to the other breeds. Basenjis were confident and scored well at first, but then seem to lose motivation. Fox Terriers tended to try to bite their way out.

The point here is that different breeds perform in different ways depending on the task and the training method. Because of differences in breed-typical reactions and abilities, there's no single test of intelligence that is fair among breeds.

Obedience competition. A breed's perceived trainability is influenced by the expectations and training methods of the people who acquire them. Few people with a strong interest in obedience competition buy a bottom-ranked breed as their next prospective obedience trial champion. Yet these are the very people who have the knowledge to best train a dog. When gifted trainers have taken up the challenge, these so-called least trainable breeds have excelled.

Perhaps these overachievers were flukes. Individual differences do outshine breed differences. Do such unusually trainable dogs produce unusually trainable offspring? Probably. Selection schemes undertaken by military and guide dog breeding organizations have produced more trainable dogs through generations.

If your goal is to have an obedient, competition dog, you'll do well to choose a breed regarded as highly trainable and a dog from an obedience-star-studded pedigree. If your goal is to succeed in obedience with the breed you already love, you'll do best to remain optimistic, accept your dog's natural inclinations, use a training technique most suited for your breed—and keep a good sense of humor! Either way, you can justify getting one of those bumper stickers that proclaims "My dog is smarter than your honor student."

Are They Outgoing?

How many times have you heard somebody with an adopted dog attest that the dog must have been abused because he's so shy? It's possible. It's also possible his abuse was more benign, stemming not so much from actual abuse but as neglect and failure to socialize. It is also possible he is shy because that's his nature.

Hereditary shyness. Another large-scale dog genetic study took place in the 1930s. Dogs of various breeds were crossed and their behavior and other traits were measured. The researchers eventually noticed they had a lot of very shy dogs, and when they looked at these dogs' pedigrees they found they had something in common: they all traced back to one very shy Basset Hound.

It would be 50 more years before the genetics of shyness in dogs was rigorously examined. A family of nervous Pointers was maintained for generations. Even if raised by and socialized alongside outgoing Pointers, these nervous Pointers freeze when approached by a stranger. Not every dog from a nervous family is equally nervous. The dogs can become slightly less nervous with training, with bird dog training in the field helping most. In another line of shy dogs (this time Huskies) currently being studied, socialization is more effective.

Bold versus shy. One aspect of domestication is selection against shyness and for boldness. A continuum of shyness to boldness is found both within wolves and dogs, with some dog breeds tending to be bolder or shyer as a whole. Bold dogs are easier to train as working dogs, regardless of task, but they aren't always the best choice for pets because a certain amount of caution is advantageous.

Breeders can select for shyness or for boldness, but environment also has considerable influence. Even a dog from the boldest background will never be bold if he doesn't receive early socialization. Every dog's temperament is a reflection of its genetic heritage and experience. Not every shy dog has been abused, just as not every abused dog is shy.

Are They Friendly?

We expect our dogs to act with Lassie-like, or at least Gandhi-like, benevolence. Yet there's a truth we must acknowledge: dogs are dogs, and dogs will act aggressively at times. That's one reason humans selected them as their best friends. Perhaps Plato put it best 2,000 years ago:

"The disposition of noble dogs is to be gentle with people they know and the opposite with those they don't know...."

All dogs can be aggressive to some extent and under certain circumstances. The acceptable degree and circumstances will differ from owner to owner and according to the dog's function. Unfortunately some misinformed owners and trainers believe aggressive dogs are necessary to perform guardian functions, when in fact, truly aggressive dogs are not sufficiently trustworthy or controllable to perform as reliable guards.

A mean gene? Are dogs really born mean? Are some breeds more likely to be man killers? Some jobs require higher degrees of assertiveness or aggression. But most scientists agree there's no such thing as a mean gene—although one discovery comes tantalizingly close. Some animals (there's no dog data yet) with low levels of an enzyme that affects chemicals important to behavior have a greater tendency to behave aggressively compared to those with normal levels. But genes don't work in a vacuum: men with low levels of this enzyme who have deficient childhoods tend to become violent adults, whereas those from nurturing childhoods do not. Men with normal levels do not tend to become violent no matter what their upbringing. Thus, as with all things behavioral, it is the interaction between genes and the environment that is the major determinant.

Canine aggression is costly and potentially deadly. According to fatal attack statistics, between 38 and 50% of fatalities can be attributed to two breeds. But about thirty-six different breeds, including some known for being affable, have also been responsible for fatalities. Aggressive behavior is one of the most common reasons people take their dogs to clinical behaviorists for help. Most of them blame themselves for their dog's behavior, but mounting evidence suggests the dog would have aggressive tendencies no matter how it was raised. That doesn't mean the behavior can't be prevented if detected early enough, or treated if detected later.

D-N-A and the D-O-G

The recently completed Canine Genome map of dog DNA will provide opportunities for researchers to compare human and canine genes, allowing for more behavior genes to be pinpointed. In 1999, the first such gene, called D4DR, was identified. This gene has been related to novelty-seeking behavior in humans. In comparing two breeds generally acknowledged to differ in scores of reactivity, the more reactive breed was found to have more of the long-D allele than the generally less reactive breed.

To Thine Own Self Be True

Choosing the ideal canine soul mate is going to take some soul-searching. You need to separate the person you think you are, or once were, or want to be, from the person you really are now. You may think you are a person who values independence, but will you really feel that way when your dog is blowing you off once again? You may have once been a person who could handle a giant dog, but are you still physically capable of doing so twenty years later? You may want to be a sportsperson or jogger, but do you really think getting an overly active dog will make you into one?

Everybody has a tendency to overestimate the time and effort they will spend on a dog. Getting a dog that does not fit your current lifestyle is not fair to either of you. You need to consider size, exercise requirements, activity level, grooming requirements, health problems, and climate caveats, as well as tendencies to obey, bark, herd, hunt, or do whatever they were bred to do.

Starting on the Right Paw

Before your puppy comes to live with you, he will be spending some important formative weeks with his dam, littermates, and breeder. The way he is raised even in these early weeks will have some important implications for his future behavior. That's why choosing a conscientious breeder is a vital part of choosing a puppy. Conscientious breeders:

- only sell puppies to people they have met and interviewed. That means that puppies sold through third parties probably aren't from good breeders.

- question you about your facilities, your prior experiences with dogs, and your intentions regarding your new dog. That means that sources who only ask about your credit card number probably aren't good breeders.

- breed only one or two breeds of dogs, so they can concentrate on just those breeds.

- breed no more than a few litters per year, so they can concentrate on those litters.

- can discuss their breed's health and temperament concerns.

- have clean, healthy, friendly adults.

- have clean facilities that promote interaction with their dogs.

- raise their litters inside the house and underfoot, not in a secluded kennel or garage.

- insist upon taking the dog back should you be unable to keep it at any time during its life.

Puppy mills. You will note that commercial puppy outlets cannot meet even a fraction of these requirements. Because they get their puppies from large-scale breeding operations known as puppy mills, the puppies from these sources already have the odds stacked against them.

Puppy mills tend to breed with profit as the bottom line. As such, breeding stock is seldom screened for health or temperament problems. Puppies are usually raised in overcrowded and filthy conditions, often on wire. Because they grow up relieving themselves where they happen to be and then living in it these puppies may tend to continue dirty habits as adults.

Between 3 and 5 weeks of age, puppies begin approaching people. But in a puppy mill, there is nobody to approach. A caretaker may come and throw some food in occasionally, but with hundreds of puppies there is scant time for interaction. Puppies raised in puppy mills are analogous to babies raised in overcrowded orphanages and institutions. Children growing up under such conditions may have their basic needs met, but because their caretaking is done according to the caretaker's schedule rather than in response to the child's actions, these children do not develop normal emotional responses. They become passive and cannot deal effectively with stressful situations. They also fail to develop intellectually. Years ago, when orphans were more commonly raised this way, those from overcrowded institutions often tested as mentally handicapped. In a landmark study, some of these supposedly mentally handicapped children were placed with institutionalized adults who lavished attention upon them. The children's IQ scores rose to the average range and they went on to live productive lives, in contrast to those children that never received nurturing. Like children, puppies need nurturing in order to develop normally. Puppies raised in cages without control over their environment and minimal contact with human caregivers may have difficulty being all that they could be.

Age of consent. A puppy's initial socialization period is between 3 and 5 weeks of age. At this time they learn to play and interact with littermates. As their play progresses, they display early versions of stalking, pouncing, fighting, and sexual behavior. Although they bite one another, at this age they appear to develop an inhibition against biting hard, and this experience may be necessary for the development of bite inhibition as adults. Puppies that don't play with other dogs during this stage tend to bite more forcefully when grown. Orphan pups may have to be mildly (very mildly—this is a tiny puppy here) reprimanded at this age for biting too vigorously. Pups removed from their litter too early may not only lack bite inhibition, but may suffer from a number of social and emotional problems. These may include separation distress, overreactivity, fearfulness, or aggressiveness. This is why it's important to know if a pup has grown up with littermates.

As puppies approach 7 weeks of age, some of their initial fearlessness begins to wane. They are still curious and relatively fearless, and they approach strangers optimistically. But during the next few weeks that optimism and trust will gradually fade. This is why 7 to 8 weeks of age has long been touted as the ideal time to place a puppy in its new home.

Many breeders feel 7 weeks is too early to uproot a pup from its canine family, however. If these breeders take on the responsibility of exposing the puppy to various situations and events (page 75), then the puppy should develop just as well as if he went home with you.

What about adults? Puppies are a huge responsibility and demand a tremendous amount of time and work. They can also inflict a tremendous amount of damage. Don't neglect the idea of getting an adult dog. You will have a better idea of how his personality will turn out because he is closer to the finished product.

Puppy Aptitude Testing

What if you could predict a puppy's behavior as an adult? That's the idea behind puppy aptitude tests. Originally devised for screening service dog candidates, the tests were modified and have been used on thousands of puppies. They have only one drawback: they don't appear to work.

Puppy aptitude tests are performed at 7 weeks of age, before many behaviors have a chance to develop. Many such behaviors, such as dominance-related aggression, don't appear until social maturity at around two years of age. The fact that a 7-week-old pup does not display such behaviors is not indicative that they won't appear. Nor do these tests take into account the influence of later environmental factors.

These tests do have their place in discovering problems that are already present, such as unusually aggressive, resistant, or shy behaviors. This gives the breeder a chance to place such puppies with careful, experienced owners—and gives owners the knowledge of what to work on. Puppy aptitude tests are useful, but don't use them to choose between two otherwise similar puppies without obvious behavior problems.

Meet your match. You should, however, use your common sense in evaluating puppy temperaments. Arrange to spend at least a half hour or more with a prospective dog or puppy. Ask the breeder about their personalities. The breeder will know more about them than you will be able to deduce in your limited time. Ask about the pup's typical behavior, and if the pup is acting unusually calm or active at the moment.

It's hard not to be impressed with the pup that is a little spitfire, or want to nurture the one who shyly hangs back. Unless you have a fondness for naughty dogs or one-person dogs, you'd do better to pick the pup that plays a little, comes to say "Hi," then nestles in your lap when he's finally exhausted. Let's face it, in most litters it's hard not to try to fit every pup in your car and take them all home. But if you don't see the pup of your dreams, tell the breeder. A good breeder only wants you to leave with a puppy that has captured your heart.

Waifs and Strays

Maybe you've studied and finally chosen the perfect breed for you. But then fate intervenes. Some other dog shows up on your doorstep and asks to stay just a while. He inserts himself into your life and burrows into your heart despite what your head is telling you. "Just a while" becomes a lifetime—and you never knew how you managed without him. That's the romantic side of rescue.

The reality is that adopting a rescue, while bringing special rewards, may also entail special challenges. Chances are he's not the product of a responsible breeding program aimed at producing stable temperaments and health. He probably hasn't been raised using the latest dog psychology. He hasn't eaten the finest in canine nutrition. He may come with a host of behavioral problems. Accommodating him into your lifestyle may be a bigger challenge than welcoming a dog of your choice, but you may be his last chance. Some rescue dogs may be better off with a more experienced owner. Some owners may be better off with a dog with no baggage. But sometimes all it takes is giving fate a chance, and you find you have a match made in heaven.

"Money will buy you a pretty good dog, but it won't buy the wag of his tail."

—Unknown

Chapter 3
Language Skills

Congratulations! You're going to learn a new language!

Imagine the tables were turned and your dog got to train you for a day. He could probably train you to cook him a steak and drive him around in the car (actually, he probably already has), but when he tried to train you to help him sniff out some moles you would be a dismal failure. He would have to conclude you were stupid or stubborn. The same thing happens when we ask our dogs to do something they can't comprehend.

Making Sense

You and your dog share the same physical world, but you live in two different sensory worlds. Even when you and your dog both perceive the same thing, you often interpret it very differently.

Your dog's wolf heritage has formed his sensory world. He evolved as a hunter, detecting prey by scent, sight, and sound. He evolved as a social animal, communicating with his pack through olfactory, visual, and auditory signals. His sense of taste ensured that he sought out nutritious food and avoided bad food. His sense of touch helped him avoid injury and seek comfort.

Communication. Once dogs joined people in their world, it appears they evolved to understand human gestures to some extent. Research suggests that dogs are the best of any non-human animal at understanding our gestures. Even so, they must be in a constant state of confusion from our crazed, and, to them, unnatural output. Why are we hugging them? Dogs don't hug. Why are we calling them yet standing facing them? Those are mixed messages to dogs. Why are we slathering ourselves with vile-smelling perfumes yet washing the sweet smell of rotting flesh from their fur? People just don't make sense.

We communicate all day long with our dogs, babbling an endless stream of words. We feel as though our dogs understand us because they cock their heads knowingly. Of course, the head is cocked trying to detect one of the magically important words such as "walk" or "eat" while we pour out our troubles to them. But even that response is reassuring. Who else could give us such an unequivocal "Yes" when we ask "So do you think I should go for Walt?"

We also communicate through gesture and touch. We have a hard time talking to our dogs without waving our arms around, bending over, and adding facial expressions. And we all feel we can read our dogs—or at least we think we know what a wagging tail means. We think we know when and where our dogs like to be touched, and we certainly enjoy caressing them. But we're not always right with our gestures or assumptions. We put most of the burden of this inter-species communication on the member that's supposed to be the less intelligent one. Shouldn't we at least be trying to meet them halfway?

Talk Doggy to Me

You know it's happened to you: You call your dog's name in an effort to have him come; he glances up at you, and then goes on about his business. So you call louder: "BUBBA!" No response. So you try again: "Now!" "Get over here!" "Right here!" "Come!" "I mean it!" "Come on boy!" "Come, *come*, COME!" No response. No surprise.

There's no need to shout. It's no accident dogs make good burglar alarms and hunters. Your dog can hear the rustle of a prowler outside in the driveway. He can hear the squeak of a mouse in a wall. He can hear your car returning home long before it pulls into view. Then what makes you think he can't hear his name called from across the yard?

Do You Hear What I Hear?

Your dog can hear mid-range noises about four times farther away than you can. He can hear high-pitched sounds you can't hear at any distance. That's why dogs can hear dog whistles and you can't. It's also why they can hear some ultrasonic pest and flea repellers, which must be very annoying to them.

Some dogs, particularly spotted white dogs with no color around their ears, are prone to deafness. Dalmatians are the best-known dog breed with hereditary deafness, but many other dogs are also deaf in one or both ears. Some dogs may become deaf from old age, drugs, or exposure to loud noises.

If you suspect your dog is deaf, try this simple test: Stand behind your dog or in another room and say something or make a noise your dog normally responds to. Make sure he can't see you out of the corner of his eye or in a reflection, or can't feel any vibrations or air currents from your movements. If he doesn't respond, try again, this time using a startling noise such as a hand clap. He should twitch an ear or turn his head. If he doesn't, wait until he's panting and try one more time. Most dogs will stop panting for a second to hear an interesting sound better. Of course, he will soon tire of all this and just learn to ignore you altogether, so don't push it too much. If he never responds, talk to your veterinarian about having a BAER (brainstem auditory evoked response) hearing test done.

If your dog is deaf, you can still communicate with him through his other senses. You can thump on the floor to get his attention and then use hand signals to tell him what you want. You can call him in the dark by blinking a flashlight, and you can even use a radio-controlled vibrating collar to get his attention at a distance.

Words. It's not that your dog can't hear you; it's more likely he can't understand you. For one thing, if you're like most people, you called to him first of all by just shouting his name. That may have gotten his attention, but then you never told him what you wanted. When you did finally get around to telling him, you gave him too many variations on the theme. Your dog doesn't have a built-in thesaurus. It's hard enough to teach him one word for one behavior; why push it?

When we speak to children who don't respond, we naturally try speaking louder (which usually just makes them cry) or we try different words that they might better understand. We run them together in sentences and change their order, but when we do this with dogs we forget that dogs don't use grammar. This lack of grammar ability causes them even more problems when we try to influence their behavior by stringing words together. If your dog knows what "Bark" means and what "No" means, "No bark" won't tell him not to bark. "Stop barking" won't work any better. If you want him to be quiet, teach him a separate command: "Quiet."

Choose one word per desired behavior, and use it consistently. Be careful in the words you choose as cues. If you say "Down" to tell your dog to get in a down position, what is he to think when you say "Down" to tell him to get off the sofa he is already lying down on?

Say your cue word only once. Repeating it only confuses the dog about what the real cue is. Is it "Come?" or is it "Come, come, COME!" Don't expect your dog to read your mind.

Tone. Just as important as the words you choose is the inflection you use. Dogs don't read. They hear your words as sounds, not as vowels and consonants that mean the same thing no matter how they are said. Choose a way of saying each cue and stick with it.

In almost every species, high-pitched sounds are made by infants and juveniles, and are often used by adults when yelling out in fear or in play. They make the recipient feel playful or dominant. Low-pitched sounds indicate power, aggression, and leadership, and are often used as threats. They make the recipient take notice.

The tone you choose depends on the type of behavior you're trying to get. It's natural to speak to dogs, especially puppies, in the same high-pitched voice that parents around the world use with their babies. This baby talk tends to encourage both babies and dogs to interact and play. It's non-threatening, but because of that, it's easy to ignore. That's one reason drill sergeants don't call out commands in high-pitched kootchie-cooing baby talk. It's also why you don't want to use baby talk when you're trying to get your dog to stop doing something. If your dog is getting ready to run into the road, it's time to lower your voice into your "I mean business" gruff command mode and yell out "STOP!"

Do dogs use these tones with each other? In general, higher-pitched sounds, such as those puppies make, are associated with subordinate intentions, and lower-pitched sounds, such as big animals make, are associated with dominant intentions. If a dog wants mercy, he yelps like a puppy. If he wants to sound threatening, he growls with his lowest-pitched voice.

Cadence. Besides words and tone, the cadence of what you say influences how your dog responds. This seems to be a universal rule with animals and how they respond to human voice commands throughout the world. We even use it when talking to each other or to children.

- If we're trying to slow or calm a person or dog, we use long, drawn-out, quiet, monotone commands: "Eaaassy," "Staaaaaaay," or "Doown."

- If we're trying to stop a person or dog quickly, we use a low-pitched abrupt sound: "NO!" "Aghht!" "Stop!"

- If we're trying to encourage or hurry a person or dog, we use a series of short, repeated high-pitched sounds that continue to rise in pitch "Go, go, go, go, go!" "Here, pup, pup, pup, pup, pup!"

Most of us naturally do use these cadence changes. That's why the typical home-raised puppy is really convinced his name is "Puppuppuppuppup." Either that or "No!"

You know better than to name your dog something like "Nomad" that can be confused with "No" or "Bad." You should also consider how his name will sound when you call him. It may be hard to call out "Rover" in a way that speeds your dog up, or "Peppy" in a way that slows him down.

Strong Language

Here's another reason your dog may not be coming when you're calling: Your voice may be saying "Come" but your body may be saying "Go." And for most dogs, body language trumps verbal language.

Dogs are adept at noticing our body language, but unfortunately our intentions are often lost in translation.

- In our culture, looking somebody directly in the eye is a sign of sincerity. In dog culture, it's a threat.

- In our culture, striding right up to somebody to make introductions is considered polite. In dog culture, it's the height of rudeness.

- In our culture, bending forward is only natural when we try to call a child to us. In dog culture, it pushes them away.

- In our culture, slapping somebody on the back or tousling them on top of the head is a sign of affection. In dog culture, it's a statement of dominance.

- In our culture, hugging somebody is a way to make them feel more secure. In dog culture, it makes them uncomfortable.

Decoding Dog Talk

Dogs use barks, howls, whines, growls, and a variety of other sounds to communicate with each other. Use this doggy lexicon to figure out what your dog is saying:
- Growl of low pitch: warning to a subordinate to go away
- Growl of low pitch, often including sharp barks: warning or threat to an equal to stay away
- Growl of high or undulating pitch: warning of a fearful or uncertain dog
- Growl of high pitch, short duration, and frequent repetition: playful growl

- Repeated "rough" sounding exhalation while playing: canine equivalent of laughter

- Single short bark or yip: demanding signal
- Single low-pitch bark: warning to an equal to stay away
- Repeated quick barks: intruder alert
- Repeated yips: excitement barks, often occurring during play
- Single soft bark: invitation to play or first uncertain warning bark

- Howl with yip: used when a family member leaves or arrives
- Howl: may indicate loneliness

Grrrrrrrr...

If you have several dogs, you will probably hear some grumbling and growling going on between them. Some people try to put an end to this, but grumbling and growling is a dog's way of complaining and warning. You wouldn't expect to have several children and never have them throw complaints and threats back and forth. Let your dogs tell each other what's bothering them (to a reasonable extent) and what's going to happen unless the other one quits. If you train your dog not to complain or warn, he may instead just attack the other without warning.

How not to greet. So let's see how a typical man-meets-dog scenario goes. You're walking your dog down the street trying to socialize him. Up strides a stranger, who calls to your dog while staring him in the eye, all the while walking straight up to him. In your dog's mind, this guy is giving off threats. Only a dominant dog would approach quickly and frontally, and especially only a dominant dog would do so while staring the other in the eye. The stranger then bends over your dog. In dog language, the act of "standing over," in which a dog stands over a reclining dog or places his neck over the withers of another dog, are declarations of dominance. The stranger then reaches out to touch your dog on the head. Dogs don't pet each other. If a strange dog places a foot on another's back, it's to show he's boss. It's often a prelude to a fight or to mounting. "Good dog!" the stranger exclaims, adding a couple of hearty slaps to your dog's ribs. Another challenge! The last straw comes when our friendly but clueless stranger tries to show how loving he is by giving your dog a big hug. Dogs don't hug. The only time one dog wraps his arm around another is when mounting or fighting. At this point your dog either tries to escape or snaps in self-defense. You are mortified; why would your dog act this way when the stranger was only trying to be nice? Not in your dog's mind. This guy was clearly threatening and dominating. With time, dogs come to realize we humans are social idiots, and they can learn to accept our ways. To an extent.

How to greet. Wouldn't it be preferable if people could learn to move around dogs in ways that truthfully communicated their friendly intentions? To greet a strange dog on his terms, turn sideways to the dog and stop. Don't stare into his eyes. Give the dog a chance to approach and meet you halfway. Don't lean over him; if you want to get to his level, kneel down, preferably still facing sideways to him. For a shy dog, face away from him. Don't pet the dog on the top of his head or body; if you must touch, scratch him under his neck or on his forechest. And save your hugs and kisses for your own dog who feels more comfortable with you.

How to call. What about those conflicting signals you're giving when calling your dog? Wolves and dogs are adept at following the direction in which their pack leader is headed. They pay attention to the way other pack members' heads and feet are facing, and they face the same way. That's what keeps packs moving together. When the leader turns around, the followers stop. When the leader advances on them, the followers turn around and start walking in the opposite direction, away from the leader. It's as though the leader had a force field that pushes away followers in front of him and pulls followers behind him. If a wolf leader wants another to follow, he turns and walks away. It works like a charm.

But people do the opposite. When the average person (the dog's leader) wants her dog to come, she faces him. The dog naturally stops. She calls, leaning forward. He takes a few steps back. So she walks toward the dog to go get him. He walks away. Frustrated, she gives up and decides to just turn around and go on without the obviously spiteful beast. Voila! He trots along beside her.

Dogs can learn to ignore your conflicting signals, but it's easier for you to learn not to give them. If you really want your dog to come, don't just face away—walk, or better, run away! If you have to stay in place, lean backward, not forward. In a pinch, make yourself little by lying flat on the ground. Few dogs can resist that, although for obvious reasons it's not the recall method of choice for public places.

Stop! If you want your dog to stop in his tracks, turn abruptly and face him, rising to your full height, even raising your arms. Make yourself look big. If he still creeps to you submissively, move toward him.

Dogs use body language to control one another all the time. They use their body to block the path of another dog if they don't want that dog to go somewhere. You can do this too, by simply stepping into the path of your dog. Even leaning forward slightly as though you intend to step there will tend to push your dog back.

In the ring. If you compete in obedience or agility trials, you will learn to make the most of your body language. Point your toes and body in the direction you want your dog to go. Don't twist your trunk to watch your dog while heeling, and be sure your feet and body are pointing to the obstacle you want your dog to tackle in agility. Don't lean forward when you call your dog; instead, lean slightly back. Remember that, in general, leaning toward your dog pushes him away. Since body language is discouraged in obedience trials, practice at home being poker-faced and poker-bodied. The first few times, your dog is likely to suddenly stop obeying you. Better to find that out at home than in the ring. Countless dogs have failed to stay during the long sit and down exercises at trials because of mixed messages from their handlers. It's common for a handler to stare at her dog, as though using laser beams to glue him into position. The more the handler stares, the more uncomfortable the dog becomes. Uncomfortable dogs tend to slink to their leaders in appeasement. Be sure to look to the side of your dog during the stay exercises.

It's not only in the ring that your messages may suddenly change. If you usually act like the village idiot when you play and train your dog at home, don't expect him to respond as usual if you suddenly feel inhibited in public. Gone are your exaggerated arm movements and goofy grin—after all, people are watching! The problem is, so is your dog, and he has no idea how to interpret "wooden." You'll have to train your dog to attend more to your verbal cues than physical ones; either that, or abandon any sense of pride and act like a fool in public, too.

Leader language. In general, lowered body postures are associated with submissive intentions and high, direct body postures with dominant intentions. If you want to help a dog relax, avoid quick movements, but also avoid slow, deliberate movements, which look too much like stalking. Just move easily and naturally. If you want a dog to perceive you as a leader, stand up straight and walk briskly.

Children and wrong messages. Children are more often bitten by dogs because they do things that alarm or excite dogs. They tend to run toward strange dogs, often throwing their arms around them for a hug before the dog is comfortable with them. Face to face with a wary dog, the dog may snap, biting the child in the face. Children often run and play, screeching in a high pitch that sounds like an injured prey animal. When frightened by a dog, they run directly away and scream, awakening a dog's prey drive. Either circumstance can elicit chase behavior in dogs that are not familiar with children. Although these are not excuses for dogs that bite, they are a reality, and children should be coached on how to act around dogs. By the same token, be aware that most children don't behave appropriately around dogs, even with coaching, and your dog needs to get used to how these small humans behave.

Consistency. You may have coached other members of your family on which verbal cues to use, but what about their body language? You all need to be consistent in that, as well. It's hard not to gesture when talking to your dog, but at least try to get all family members gesturing to him the same way.

Facial expressions. Just as you pay attention to facial expressions, so does your dog. Dogs learn to understand smiling, but if you show a lot of teeth it can intimidate an uneasy dog. A direct stare will make a dog uncomfortable. A furrowed brow is interpreted as anger by both dogs and humans. Dogs are so adept at reading facial expressions that one reason people claim their dog "knows he's done something wrong" is that the dog picks up on the owner's angry expression and then tries to act submissively in appeasement.

Reading dog signals. Giving off the right signals is only half the battle. Reading your dog's signals is the other half. Unfortunately, we humans are just as bad at that. When the stranger in the earlier example approached your dog, you should have noticed how your dog leaned backwards, plastered his ears down, and tucked his tail. If you noticed you would have realized your dog was scared. Maybe you should have noticed your dog's pupils dilating and the corners of his mouth moving ever so slightly forward. If you had, maybe you would have realized your dog was ready to bite. Had you noticed you might have realized your dog was afraid, trapped, and about to bite out of fear, and you would have cautioned the stranger to back off. Instead, the dog snapped when the stranger tried to hug him, and the dog was accused of biting without warning. Yet he gave every warning he could; you and the stranger, "Mr. Ihavawaywithdogs," just ignored them.

Do You See What I See?

Dogs need good vision to read our body language. But just what can they see? Vision may be the one sense where we have the upper hand over our dogs—sort of. We can see fine details our dogs can't see, and our range of color vision is greater. Dogs have color vision like people who are typical red-green color-blind; that is, they can tell blue from yellow but confuse reds, oranges, yellows, and greens. Even though dogs do see colors, they don't seem to pay a lot of attention to them. But dogs have the advantage when it comes to seeing in dim light and discerning slight movements. It's this ability to notice our slight facial gestures that we often don't give them credit for, yet it turns out that dogs are accomplished readers of subtle changes of facial expressions and body language.

Dog Body Language Lexicon

The next time you go to a dog park or other places where dogs interact, look for dogs with the following body and facial language. Then study your own dog and see how he uses his body language to communicate.

- Dog advancing: indicates dominance or aggression
- Dog retreating: indicates fear or anxiety
- Dog facing squarely: indicates confidence, dominance, or aggression
- Dog standing sideways: indicates confidence without asserting dominance

- Body leaning forward: indicates confidence and interest
- Body leaning forward with stiff-legged stance: indicates dominance or aggressive intention
- Body leaning backward: indicates fear or submission
- Body or head lowered: indicates fear, anxiety, or submission
- Body or head lowered and twisted: indicates submission
- Body lowered on front end only: indicates playfulness
- Body lowered on ground and upside down: indicates extreme submission or fear
- Body upside down and rolling: indicates pleasure
- Hackles raised: indicates arousal associated with aggression or fear
- Paw placed on another's back: indicates dominance or aggression
- Head and neck placed over another's back: indicates dominance or aggression
- Shoulder or hip slam into another: indicates dominance or playfulness
- Head turned away: indicates submission or a truce
- Head held high, arched neck: indicates confidence or challenge

- Tail held horizontal or naturally: indicates interest
- Tail raised, held stiffly, and quivering: indicates dominance or aggressive intention
- Tail tucked: indicates fear, anxiety, or submission
- Tail tucked but wagging: indicates submission
- Tail wagging slowly but broadly: indicates relaxation, playfulness, or anticipation
- Tail wagging quickly and broadly: indicates submission or pleasure

- Ears forward: indicates interest, dominance, playfulness, or aggression
- Ears back: indicates fear
- Ears down: indicates submission

- Eyes opened wide and staring: indicates aggression
- Eyes turned away and squinting: indicates submission
- Eyes blinking rapidly: indicates stress
- Eyes with dilated pupils: indicates arousal, often from fear or aggression

- Mouth agape with lip corner forward: indicates aggression
- Mouth slightly open with lip corner pulled back, all teeth showing: indicates fear
- Mouth open with lip corner pulled upward, often with tongue showing: indicates relaxation or playfulness
- Mouth licking the air or toward you or another dog rapidly: indicates submission
- Mouth licking lips: may indicate stress or anticipation of eating
- Face, nose, or lips wrinkled, teeth showing: indicates aggression
- Front teeth showing but no signs of aggression: indicates submission (the "canine grin")
- Mouth yawning: indicates nervousness or serves to reduce tension in aggressive situations
- Muzzle push: indicates submission, affection
- Panting: if not hot or tired, may indicate anxiety or pain

Scent of a Canine

You've traveled hundreds of miles to take your dog vacationing with you, and you've finally arrived at your destination: the Grand Canyon. As you call him to share the awe-inspiring view, he can't be bothered. He's found something really worthy of attention: a pile of poop. If dogs showed slide shows of their vacations, they would be scent slides of the deer poop they found in Arizona, the fox urine they sniffed in Alabama, and the dead seal they rolled on in Alaska. Now that's what doggy memories are made of!

Our dogs must be baffled as we drag them away from an intriguing scent post full of information about the neighborhood dogs. They must be repulsed as we slather overpowering perfumes on our bodies and spray vile air fresheners around our rooms. They must be bewildered when we don gloves and wash the rotted carcass and raccoon poop out of their coats. And they must be perplexed that we seem so stupid, so blind, when it comes to their rich world of scent.

Pee-mail. Dogs can tell what dogs have been posting pee-mail and whether that pee-mail is inviting them over for a tryst or telling them this property is labeled "No Trespassing." Not only do they get information from smelling urine, but also from licking it up. Your dog may lick up a small sample of urine and then chomp his jaws slowly up and down, sometimes foaming a bit at the mouth at the same time. He is not a pervert. He is doing this to force a bit of the urine into a special sensory organ that's located in the roof of his mouth. This organ, the vomeronasal organ, tells your dog the sexual status of the urine sample-giver. Intact male dogs are especially likely to sample urine; it's sort of like reading a girlie magazine or visiting an online dating site.

Mine! Dogs use urine to mark what they consider to be their territory. When you walk your dog around the neighborhood and allow him to lift his leg at will on every post, you give him an inflated idea of what his territory is. Some behaviorists have advocated that owners of dog-aggressive dogs should curtail their dog's marking in order to remove that sense of territory. However, studies have not yet supported the effectiveness of this treatment.

Dogs will also mark over the urine of other dogs, especially those they consider to be their subordinates. If you're trying to keep your dog out of your garden, you may try spreading the urine of a dominant animal around it. Of course, this may just backfire and entice him to urinate near it, so don't get too carried away at first. Dogs will urinate in the general vicinity of where they have urinated before, which is why it's so important to prevent your dog from revisiting areas inside the house where he may have urinated. Some people claim success encouraging puppies to urinate outside by modeling the behavior for them when the neighbors aren't looking! Or maybe that was just the excuse they gave when they were caught.

Intact (and sometimes, castrated) males may mark inside your home. This is a difficult habit to stop. They will tend to avoid marking areas that smell of moth balls, but how do you hang mothballs on your walls and furniture in a way that is both decorative and difficult for your dog to eat? Want to get rich? Create a spray odorless to humans that will dissuade male dogs from marking indoors.

Sniff, Sniff

You can tell when your dog is actively smelling something because he takes lots of short, shallow sniffs rather than long, deep breaths. Different breeds probably vary greatly in the ability to smell. In general, dogs with long, deep noses have many more olfactory receptor cells than do those with flat noses, and probably have a better sense of smell.

My card. Dogs get to know each other by first sniffing at each others genitals, anus, mouth corners, and ears, all areas that produce a good deal of scent. Of these, the genitals tend to elicit the most interest. When meeting new people, dogs also go for the crotch. It's not because they are oversexed. They are simply reading "your card," so to speak. Of course, that doesn't mean you have to stand for it. A submissive dog has to stand there and let his superior sniff him; you don't. Simply move away, face sideways to the dog, have him sit, and then reward him for polite behavior.

The smell of fear. Dogs also leave powerful scent signals through anal sac secretions. Some of these secretions are forced out whenever the dog defecates, imparting extra, and presumably individualized, scents to the feces (as though it wasn't already smelly enough). When dogs are extremely frightened, they expel their anal sacs to produce a musky smell that instantly elicits intense interest from other dogs. Even we can smell it, but we tend to run the other way. Its exact function is unknown, but some researchers believe it acts to dispel aggression in other dogs. Other dogs will show great interest in the secretions, and probably get a message that the sender had something terrifying occur in that spot.

Many people have proposed that dogs can "smell fear," although no research exists to support this. People fortunately do not have anal sacs, but it's not unreasonable to believe people may produce certain chemicals when alarmed. It's also likely that dogs can detect the slight increase in our body odor that accompanies our increased sweat when we're nervous. Dogs have such an adept sense of smell that they can detect skin and bladder cancer in people, can tell people apart through scent, and can follow scent trails that are several days old. For them to detect slight changes in our body chemistry should present little challenge.

Dog Appeasing Pheromones

Mammalian dams produce an odor, or pheromone, from the area of their breasts when lactating that seems to appease their young. Studies of rats and farm animals have shown that juveniles and adults exposed to these pheromones become much calmer and grow better. Each species has a slightly different nursing pheromone, and a commercially available dog appeasing pheromone (DAP) appears to have a calming effect on dogs.

A Touching Experience

Touch is one of the most important senses to puppies. Young puppies that are handled reap many of the same benefits that are so well documented in rats handled as pups; that is, they are more active, socially confident, and healthier as adults. When young puppies are given a choice of staying with a wire-mesh "mother" that provides milk versus a cloth one that is milkless, they will choose the cloth. When young puppies are isolated from their litter their distress calls are reduced by soft objects but not by food or hard toys.

Puppies usually sleep touching one another, and that trait remains in many adult dogs. That's one reason dogs tend to cuddle with you in bed. It gives them warmth and security, and adds an alarm system should you get up. Many dogs gradually begin to sleep alone as they get older.

Petting. Some dogs enjoy getting back rubs and side rubs, much as cats do. They'll sometimes walk along a hallway leaning against the wall or, for a double-sided rub, walk between your legs. A dog that enjoys being petted will often place his head under your hand and push up (but caution: This behavior may be a low-key attempt to control you). Your dog may get your attention by nudging you, at first softly, and then, when you're apparently too dense to get the hint, vigorously.

When adult distressed dogs are petted, their heart and breathing rates decrease and they appear calmer. Petting to calm a dog is best done using deep muscle massage with long, firm strokes reaching from the head to the rear. One of the best parts of sharing your life with a dog by your side is being able to reach over and caress his soft fur, and research has shown that doing so also reduces our heart rate and gives us a sense of well-being. Take the time to massage your dog. Not only will it do both of you good, but it will also increase bonding between you. If you have an excitable dog, teaching him to relax is one of the most important lessons he can learn.

Rub your dog's fur the right way. Most (but not all) dogs generally enjoy being massaged or rubbed. Long, slow, gentle strokes are best for calming a nervous dog, while hearty pats may invigorate a bored dog. But, as with people, there are times when being petted isn't appreciated. If your dog (or child) is playing with friends, or in the middle of a game, the last thing he wants is for Mom to come and pet him. That's just not cool!

Don't touch! One place almost every dog hates to be touched is on the feet. That's why cutting toenails can be such a challenge, and why you need to start when he is young, rewarding him for being cooperative. For some dogs it only takes one mistake of cutting the sensitive quick for them to be forever leery of your nail-cutting ability.

Dogs also have extremely sensitive vibrissae (whiskers), and may not like having them touched. Many people cut their dog's vibrissae in order to compete in conformation shows. Some anecdotal evidence exists that vibrissa-less dogs are more prone to eye injuries in the field. Cats and rats with cut vibrissae may have reduced balancing ability, but no such data exists for dogs.

Status. Dogs often touch each other to convey status. Placing a paw on another's dog's back, slamming another dog with a shoulder or hip, or grabbing another dog around the neck are all ways of saying "I'm the boss in these parts, but we can play."

Most dogs don't like having strangers pet them on top of the head. Nor do they particularly enjoy being hugged. Unlike us, dogs are not natural clingers. Their front limbs are specialized for running, and they do not carry their offspring except by mouth. Hugging more often occurs as a prelude to a fight, when a dominant dog puts his paws on the back of another. When we hug our dogs it doesn't tend to make them feel secure as it does in humans. In fact, it may make them feel threatened and restricted. That's not to say your dog can't learn to enjoy being hugged, or at least held, by you. But he probably won't enjoy it if a stranger does it.

Mixed Messages

The next time you're with your dog in a tense situation, look at what you do. Chances are you start petting and rubbing your dog. If you watch almost anybody on television being interviewed about their dog, that person is usually rubbing the fur right off the poor dog's skin. It may be calming the person, but it's not calming the dog. That's a mixed message. How often do you give mixed messages?

- You tell him to come, but then stride toward him (The message he gets: "Go away").

- You tell him to stop doing something in your sweetest voice ("It's OK").

- You tell him to stop barking by yelling "Stop! I tell you, STOP! Shut up!" ("I'm barking, too!").

- You try to prevent your dog from chasing the cat he's stalking by running toward them and yelling ("Let's get her!").

- You try to stop your dog from pulling on lead by yelling "Heel, heel, heel, heel!" ("Go faster!").

- You try to calm your dog at the veterinarian's office by petting him rapidly ("Uh oh, something's up!").

- Your dog chases the delivery man's truck down the driveway and you run after him yelling "Stop! Stop! Stop!" ("Attaboy, get him! Go faster!").

- You try to make your dog stop growling at a stranger by petting the dog and speaking soothingly ("You're my protector!").

- You try to prevent your uncertain but growling dog from attacking another dog by petting him ("That's right, boy. Let's get him!").

When you mix your signals, you confuse your dog at best and very likely end up having your dog obey the wrong signal. Your dog may be smart, but he can't read your mind.

The bottom line: Try to communicate in unambiguous ways your dog innately understands. Sure, he can learn to speak your language—but why not try to at least meet him halfway?

"If dogs could talk, perhaps we'd find it just as hard to get along with them as we do people."
                                                    —*Karel Capek 1890–1938*

Chapter 4
One of the Family

Congratulations! Your new bundle of joy is coming home!

You want your dog to be a real member of your family. But he is a dog, and he's going to need a few rules that your non-furred family members may do without.

These early days are a time of great excitement for you, but great confusion for him. Be a good parent and help him through this time. The way you introduce your pup to family life will influence your puppy's behavior for years to come.

House Rules

Human babies have a big advantage over canine puppies when it comes to preparing for them. With human babies, you have nine months to get things ready, and then many more months before your baby can even use most of the stuff you bought. With canine puppies, you have only a couple of months to prepare, and once the little one has arrived, he's ready to start exploring.

If you thought teaching a child to behave indoors was hard, you haven't seen anything compared to a puppy. Your puppy has all the curiosity of a child packed in a super-athlete's body. He can gnaw, run, dig, claw, and squeeze like no child you ever want to meet. He may not draw on the walls with crayons, but he will eat them (both the walls and the crayons) and give you colored diarrhea all over your rugs if you give him a chance. Try to put a diaper on him, and he will eat that too.

Fur on the Furniture?

Some of us love having our dog lounge beside us as we relax on the sofa. A few of us even buy furniture that looks comfy for the dog. But others still cling to the idea that they can preserve their home, and they like the idea of furniture that company won't assume has fake fur upholstery. You can teach your dog it's fine to get up on the furniture anytime you want to teach him that—he'll catch on fast. But you can't easily teach him it's no longer OK to get on furniture if he's been given the go-ahead in his formative months. Your couch potato pup may have a difficult time visiting family who don't want a hairy animal on their chairs. That's why it's best to postpone furniture privileges until you are sure they will be lifelong. You can teach your dog to jump up only when his special blanket is on a piece of furniture, or when you invite him to do so. Even so, don't think he won't be wallowing amongst the sofa cushions while you're gone—he's not stupid!

Playpens for Puppies

You can't wait to start bonding with your puppy, but it seems as soon as he has a bit of freedom he's into something. What's a doggy parent to do? One solution is to set up one or more exercise pens in your favorite rooms. These portable pens serve the same function as playpens for toddlers. You can interact with your dog as you go about your business, and then let him out when you won't be distracted by other things. You can also use an exercise pen as a safe indoor yard when you have to leave him alone.

Baby gates are equally essential. Be sure you don't get the old accordion style, which can close on a puppy's neck and choke him. With a baby gate you can close your dog in a safe room but still have voice and eye contact through the open door. That way your puppy knows you haven't deserted him, and you have the added advantage of making sure he's not getting into trouble behind closed doors.

When you let your pup accompany you around the house, you can make sure he doesn't get into trouble by tying his leash around your waist. Just make sure you give him some warning before you start running to answer the phone!

A place of his own. When your puppy comes home, he wants to be with you and do everything you're doing. That includes sitting on the best furniture. Depending on his size, it may take him a while to hurl himself up there, but he'll try. There's no way for him to understand that those inviting soft cushions, perched ever so wonderfully overlooking both the house and the picture window, aren't meant just for him.

Getting up on the furniture is no cause for getting down on your pup. Simply lift him down to a place of his own. It's going to have to be a good place to compete with that sofa and its view, though. A deluxe dog bed placed in an equally entertaining spot with a good vantage point should get his attention. Teach him to go to his bed on cue by rewarding him when he goes there on his own. As he starts to eagerly run to his bed, give him the cue "Place!" and reward him once he's there (see page 127 for more explicit directions).

Overkill. Some owners resort to booby traps and shock pads to convince their dogs to stay down. These may be effective but are generally overkill. Owners who set mousetraps may find they have large veterinary bills to pay for broken toes, and those who set shock pads may find they've created dogs that are hesitant to jump anywhere or touch anything resembling such a pad. A far less traumatic dissuader is to place newspaper or another uncomfortable surface on the furniture. Most dogs will quickly decide their own bed is preferable!

Choose Your Chews

Puppies chew. Like babies, they chew when they are teething. But unlike babies, they keep on chewing. Just when you think you're safe, they seem to go through a super chewing stage as they approach their first birthday.

Nothing will teach you to be a neatnick like a chewing dog. When you do find your pup chewing on your belongings, take the object from him and replace it with a more acceptable object. Punishing him does little good, and will make matters worse if you do it right when he happens to proudly bring you the trashed treasure—because you will only teach him to take his finds to a secret location where you may never get them back. Make sure the object you give him in exchange does not resemble anything of yours you don't want him to chew. That means no old shoes! No socks, no stuffed animals (if you have children who collect them), no carpet remnants, nothing that resembles anything he can find around the house. What your puppy learns to chew on at an early age will tend to be what he looks for to chew on for the rest of his life. Choose his chews carefully.

As an extra precaution, you can slather horrible-tasting things like cayenne pepper or commercially available bitter products on your most tempting items that you can't move out of your puppy's reach. Just don't put too much confidence in them.

Better choices. Assemble a group of dog toys and only let your pup have a few at a time, rotating them every few days so he has the excitement of new toys. Be sure to include some interactive toys, such as those he must work at in order to extract food. You can fill these with bones, soft cheese, canned dog food, or peanut butter, and then freeze them to make them last even longer. Some toys dispense kibble a piece at a time as the toy is rolled. Some toys are meant to be soaked in water and frozen, providing your pup a cold teething toy. With luck, your pup will prefer these fancy toys to your fancy belongings. More likely, he'll pick something like a rope or a rag, making sure to hide the expensive toys so your friends will think you are cheap when they see that's all your poor pup has to play with.

Leave it! You can teach your pup to "Leave it!" Here's how:

1. Put a treat in your hand and show it to your dog before closing your fist over it.
2. Ignore him as he tries to get the treat from your hand. As soon as he looks away, mark the behavior (this will be explained in Chapter 9) and give him a treat from your other hand.
3. Continue until he starts to look away immediately. Then introduce the cue "Leave it" just before presenting your hand with the hidden treat.
4. Next place the treat on the floor with your foot over it. Do the same as you did with the treat in your hand. He must look away before he can have a treat in its place.
5. Once he can leave that, place the treat on the floor with a piece of screen over it.
6. Eventually your dog should be able to leave anything he encounters as soon as you say "Leave it!" because he knows he will be getting something even better from you.

Sweet Dreams

Domestic dogs are subjected to a situation that wild canids and tame children don't have to encounter: sudden removal from their family and home, the two things that give them a sense of security. The situation is far less traumatic if the breeder separates each puppy for gradually increasing time periods before they leave for their new homes, but even this may not alleviate the sudden stress of a new home.

A cry in the dark. Where will your puppy sleep at night? Before he came to your house he probably spent every night of his life snuggled in the safety of his litter. Now he has been plucked from the nest and taken to a foreign land where he knows nobody. Night falls, and he is placed in a box and left all alone. Scared and lonely, he does what any

puppy in his situation should do: he screams and cries in an attempt to be reunited with his family. Nobody comes.

You may have been told to ignore your crying puppy so you don't spoil him and reward him for crying. But what have you really taught him? You've taught him that in the most frightening situation he's ever encountered, no matter what he does, nobody is there to help him. His real mother would never treat him that way. You've taught him he is helpless, and you've taught him this at a very impressionable developmental period in his life (see page 94 for implications of learned helplessness). You have placed him in a fearful situation and refused to give him any support that may have made it more tolerable. You have taught him that being in a crate or by himself is indeed a terrifying situation. Some dog behaviorists believe such a situation may contribute to separation anxiety (page 161) in adulthood.

Traditional child-rearing advice advocated that parents ignore their crying babies, but current advice recommends comforting the baby so the baby learns she has some control over her environment. That doesn't mean you spend the rest of your life rushing in at the slightest cry, offering your child or dog a floorshow or a buffet; it means attending to their basic needs and putting them back to bed. Traditional dog-rearing advice similarly advocates ignoring the crying pup, but newer advice advocates responding in much the same way as you would to a crying baby.

Sleeping options. Choosing your pup's sleeping place, especially on those first nights, is an important decision. Sleeping outside, or in the basement or garage, is far too frightening, even if they were safe, and are not acceptable options. That leaves a small room, an ex-pen, a crate, a dog bed, or your bed.

Sleeping on the bed. Should your dog sleep on the bed? About one-third of dogs that sleep inside spend the night on the bed—despite the difficulties it sometimes causes. Sharing your bed with a dog means hairy bed sheets and being awakened during the night by your dog circling, digging, or running in place to a dream. It also means being relegated to the thinnest sliver of mattress or waking up with a twisted spine as your dog sprawls over the rest of the bed. Some studies on sleeping difficulties have shown that dogs in the bed contribute to a bad night's sleep for many people! But other die-hard dog owners nonetheless find it hard to sleep without a warm body pushing them to the edge of the bed.

Most dogs enjoy sharing your bed, but it may not be the safest place for them. Depending on your pup's size and how careful you are, you could roll over and crush him to death. He could also fall or jump out of bed, injuring himself.

Traditional trainers have cautioned that sleeping on the bed elevates the dog to a position of equality with humans, laying the groundwork for dominance issues and disobedience. But this appears not to be the case. Most dogs sleep on the bed simply because they enjoy its comfort and being next to you, not because they want to prove a point. Bed sleeping won't cause problems, although in some dogs with problems it may need to be curtailed as part of treatment. The major disadvantage to sharing your bed with your puppy is that if you later change your mind and insist he sleep elsewhere, he's not going to take it lying down.

But what about those first few nights? It's OK to loosen the rules a bit. Traditional dog trainers contend that if you let the pup into the bed this first night he'll always expect to sleep on the bed. The truth is, whether you let your pup on the bed one time, 50 times, or never, he'll always want to sleep on the bed. It's not something you have to train a dog to enjoy. Even if you don't plan to let him on the bed later, a few nights of it is really not going to make any difference. If you still don't wish to share your bed, you may wish to make your pup a bed next to yours so you can touch him as you sleep. Some people even decide to spend a couple of nights sleeping on the floor with the puppy. Regardless of what you decide, you should be close enough to comfort your pup if he cries. You are his new source of security, and he needs that now.

Sleeping in a crate. A crate is a popular choice for a doggy bed. It's safe and secure, the equivalent of a baby's crib. If your puppy is too uneasy to fall asleep all alone, let him fall asleep next to you outside the crate. When he's snoozing soundly, pick him up and place him in the crate. He may awaken momentarily but will fall back to sleep.

The crate should have plenty of soft bedding in it, as well as a stuffed toy he can use as a surrogate littermate. Keep the crate next to your bed during the next few nights until he becomes so comfortable in it he falls right to sleep. Only then should you gradually move it closer and closer to the place you wish it to remain.

As your dog gets more trustworthy, you can allow him more freedom to choose where to sleep. You may wish to place his crate in an exercise pen, and place a cuddly dog bed outside the crate so he has his choice. Once he's grown used to sleeping in his own dog bed, then you can place it beside your bed so he has a bed he can call his own. Just like a child, a dog needs his own bed and shouldn't be expected to wander around wondering where he will sleep at night. Of course, there's nothing wrong with him using his crate as his bed for as long as he wants.

Crate Training

Crates are extremely useful tools. They give your dog a secure bed of his own and give you a place to put him where you won't worry about him. Crates help in housetraining, provide a safe means of car travel, and a safe haven when staying with friends or at hotels. Every dog should be crate trained. A crate-trained dog will fare better if he has to be crated at the veterinary hospital or if he must have bed rest at home while recuperating.

But crates can be overused. They are not a place for your dog to languish while you entertain yourself with other things. Overuse of crates can create serious behavioral problems. Think of a crate as your child's crib. It's a safe place to sleep, but not a place to grow up. Nor is it a place for punishment.

Establish a good association with the crate by feeding your dog in it. At first, just place the food slightly inside the crate so he doesn't even have to go inside to eat. Then move it further inside. Finally, close the door while he eats, opening it as soon as he finishes. You can probably do this within the period of a day. Soon he will be running to the crate as soon as he sees you with food. If you want, you can now introduce a cue, such as "Kennel!" for him to go in the crate.

You can extend his time in the crate by giving him chew toys or interactive toys to occupy him while inside. Extend his time gradually, always trying to let him out before he has a chance to get bored or vocal. If he does begin to protest, wait until he is momentarily quiet before letting him out. Continue to extend the time he must be quiet before he gets released.

The crate is one of the safest spots your puppy can be, but you must do your part. Do not leave collars on puppies while they are in their crates. Collars, especially choke collars or collars with tags, can get caught in crate wires and strangle the puppy. Soft bedding is wonderful for most puppies, but those that chew and swallow it may have to be relegated to surfaces less likely to cause intestinal blockages. If your puppy tends to chew on the wire, he could get his jaw or tooth caught. Discourage such behavior by spraying the wire with anti-chew preparations and by making sure your pup has no issues with being crated.

Dog Dens

You'll often read that dogs like crates because dogs are naturally den animals. It's true that wolf cubs are den animals, but adult wolves don't live in dens. Dogs and wolves do seem to like the privacy of an enclosed space, but only if they have been introduced to such a space at a young age.

To Your Spot, Spot

Your puppy will follow you from room to room, especially if the destination is where all good smells and tastes come from, the kitchen. But a pup scampering underfoot is a sure way to topple a turkey on the floor or have similarly rewarding (for the pup) mishaps. Your pup needs a place of his own in rooms you frequent, and it's just not convenient to haul a crate from room to room. A dog bed can give him a safe spot from which to supervise your cooking. You can even teach him to go there on cue:

- First, teach him to lie down on cue (Chapter 9, page 127) on the cushion.
- Then move with him toward the cushion, tossing a treat onto the cushion from several feet away so that he bounds after it.

- As soon as he eats the treat on the cushion, tell him to lie down and give him more treats. Then have him stay for a few seconds, rewarding him with even more treats.
- Practice this sequence until he's running ahead of you to the cushion as soon as you make a throwing motion. Then throw the treat to him.
- Next, have him lie down on the cushion after he's run to it before you give him the treat. Repeat this until he is running to the cushion and lying down on his own.
- Finally introduce your cue: "To your spot!" just before you gesture toward the cushion. Keep practicing until he runs to the cushion and lies down on cue.

Don't just ignore him once he's there. He will need something to entertain himself with while there, plus you'll want to give him random treats for staying put.

Apron Strings

When you first get your new dog, it's natural to want to spend every moment with him so he will bond to you. But how do you make sure your dog is bonded to you without becoming overly dependent on you? It's important that your new dog spend time with you *and* away from you. The way you handle his time away from you will influence his ability to handle being alone as an adult.

Home alone. Moving into a new home is scary enough without being left all alone there, so it is important you get a new dog when you can be with him a lot. That doesn't mean you have to spend every waking—or sleeping—moment together. In fact, time alone is equally important.

It's natural for a young pup to seek parental security. Your pup is hardwired to become anxious if he finds himself separated from his caregiver. A puppy that finds himself all alone will give out a distress vocalization, which brings his mother on the run. If nobody shows up, he will keep crying until he is too exhausted to continue. Naïve owners may think he has gotten over his angst, but exhaustion is not the same as being OK.

This ability to scream and cry when left alone gradually increases as puppies grow up, until it finally levels off at around 7 weeks of age—

right about the time many pups are leaving for their new homes. To make matters worse, pups of this age are more likely to become distressed when left alone in an unfamiliar place.

Shut up! Many owners, nerves frayed from the puppy's ceaseless crying, resort to banging on the crate, yelling at the pup, or even giving it a swat on the butt. But studies have shown that punishment tends to make separation distress worse. After all, what does a puppy or baby who is upset want more than anything? Security. You wouldn't treat a new baby who cried all night that way; that is, not if you didn't want to be hauled off for child abuse. Instead, a good parent would comfort the baby (or maybe try to get her spouse to do so) and then walk around like a zombie all day for lack of sleep. You can always take naps at work.

I'll be right back. You want to be around to comfort your new puppy during those early transitional days, but even then you should duck out of the room occasionally. The longer you wait to introduce your pup to being alone, the harder it will ultimately be. A study that compared how pups reacted depending on whether they were first separated at either 3, 6, 9, or 12 weeks of age showed those that weren't separated until 12 weeks panicked and were unable to adjust like the other puppies could.

Your pup needs to learn that when you leave him you always return. He learns this by being left alone for very short times at first, gradually building to longer times. You may have to start by occasionally leaving the room for just a minute before popping back in. Then build up to 10, 20, and 30 minutes. Don't move on to a longer time period until your pup seems content and calm at the current time period. The object is to return before your pup gets restless or anxious.

Try your patience. Most puppies take being left alone right in stride, if it is done gradually. For those that don't, be patient. You will have made much more progress if you return while he is still calm at ten minutes than if you wait until he is having a fit at eleven minutes. The biggest barrier to getting over separation distress is being left alone too long. Nobody ever got over being scared or being deserted by being ignored. Your pup may eventually quiet down because he's too tired to continue, but he will associate being crated or left alone with being frightened. His distress is likely to build on itself, creating a lifelong problem. In fact, there's some evidence that suggests overly stressful separation may predispose dogs to later becoming hypersensitive to any stressful situation as adults, leading to a variety of fear-related behaviors.

How you leave your dog is almost as important as how long you leave him. Leave without ceremony—no long good-byes! And return without ceremony. No joyous reunions! The fact that you left and returned are not newsworthy events and it does your pup no good to convince him they are.

Security blankets. Contrary to popular opinion, crates don't seem to make young pups feel more secure. In fact, crated pups (especially those not already familiar with the crate) tend to cry even more than uncrated pups when separated. That's why it may be better to leave your pup in an exercise pen or small safe room when you first start teaching him to be home alone. You can leave a crate with an open door accessible to him in case he does prefer it.

Giving your pup something to occupy him and comfort him while you are gone is useful, but it depends on what you give. Studies have shown that mirrors and soft cuddly toys are most effective at calming separated puppies, but food has little value—probably because distressed puppies are not hungry puppies. Puppies are comforted by soft, warm, dog-shaped toys that even have a heartbeat, simulating the pup's littermates or dam.

Toys. Special interactive toys are good distractions for bored, but not distressed, puppies. These toys challenge your puppy to dislodge sticky food treats from them, occupying and rewarding them over a long time period. Remove such toys when you return (you can store them in the freezer if there's still food in them) so your dog won't already be bored with them the next time you leave. Rotating several interactive toys with different challenges will further prevent him from getting bored with them.

NOTE: If your puppy shows any evidence of chewing and swallowing bedding or toys, you may need to remove foreign materials that he could eat and use only products designed for heavy chewers.

Company. Separation distress may be helped by having another dog to keep your dog company, but you can't depend on the buddy system always being in place. You may not always have another dog, or your dog may have to spend time alone at the veterinarian's. Many dogs are not calmed by another dog.

Learning to accept being alone is an important life lesson. The tendency to suffer from full-blown separation anxiety may be inborn (page 161), but that doesn't mean you can't help your dog avoid it now.

Brain Food

It's no surprise that a balanced, nutritionally complete diet will aid in your puppy's mental development. Some recent studies have further indicated that certain fatty acids are particularly important for early learning. One of these, docosahexaenoic acid (DHA), is an important component of the nervous system, including the brain and retina, and is critical for proper mental and visual function. Human infants fed DHA have better problem solving abilities than do those not supplemented with DHA. Puppies appear to be the same. In fact, the level of DHA in puppies is partly dependent on their dam's level, especially during the last third of her pregnancy. Feeding the dam and puppies (once weaned) foods high in DHA can increase DHA levels in pups. These puppies have been shown to perform better on several tests of learning and trainability compared to pups that were not supplemented with DHA.

"A door is what a dog is perpetually on the wrong side of."
—*Ogden Nash (1902–1971)*

Chapter 5
Brave New Dog

Congratulations! You're embarking on the adventure of a lifetime!

One of the best parts of having a new young family member is taking him out to see and be seen. You'll get a lot of "oohs" and "aahs" with your human baby in her stroller, but they are nothing compared to the adoration of passersby directed at your canine puppy. As your youngster grows, you'll want to expose him to as many new situations as you feel are appropriate for his age. They call these the wonder years for children. We call them the wonder weeks for puppies.

The Wonder Weeks

It takes a lot of courage to leave the side of your mother, step from the nest, and discover the world. That's why very young puppies are relatively fearless; after all, they can't be afraid of everything new because everything is new. Besides, mom is still there to guide them. But eternally fearless dogs turn into accident-prone dogs and, ultimately, dead dogs, so nature has seen to it that as puppies age, get more active, and move away from parental influence, they also start to develop some fear of the unknown—also known as good sense.

Fools (and young puppies) rush in. Puppies start to get good sense (that is, fear) when they are only 3 weeks old. Still, they are relatively fearless of novel objects and situations, but even if something bad happens it doesn't make much of a permanent impression. The only situation that seems to distress them is being separated from their littermates or dam. Beginning at about five weeks of age, puppies start to get more cautious and remember situations or objects that weren't as fun as they looked. They begin to be more fearful of strangers, getting gradually more so week by week.

Timeline. By 7 weeks of age, pups are still relatively fearless and remain strongly attracted to new people and dogs. Because their fearfulness will continue to rise gradually, many canine behaviorists assert that the best time for puppies to go to their new homes is at 7 to 8 weeks of age, before they begin to become fearful of novel situations.

Why not bring home the new pup at an even earlier age? These early weeks are important for learning how to interact with other dogs. A puppy separated from his dam and littermates at an earlier age may not learn to inhibit his aggressive behavior properly. In addition, the dam's behavior may be important for the pups as a model of how to interact with people. Of course, if Mom is Cujo, then perhaps early separation might be advisable—but then, her not having puppies would have been an even better idea.

Deadline. The pup continues to become gradually more fearful, losing his eagerness to approach novel objects and people. Sometime after 12 weeks of age, the fear response completely swamps the approach response, making it difficult for the puppy to accept new situations it has never before experienced. This means that you have a deadline to meet, a deadline before which you need to make sure your pup has already experienced everything of significance he'll come across for the rest of his life. Of course, that's impossible, but being well socialized will put him in a better position to accept new experiences down the road.

A Shot in the Bark

There's one problem. The very best time to socialize your puppy is about the very worst time to take chances with his immunity. He may not have sufficient immunity to go trotting around town where other dogs may have shed disease. Your pup received his early immunity through his dam's colostrum during the first few days of nursing. As long as your pup still has that immunity, any vaccinations you give him won't provide sufficient immunity. But after several weeks that immunity begins to decrease. As his immunity falls, both the chance of a vaccination being effective and the chance of getting a communicable disease rise.

The problem is that immunity diminishes at different times in different dogs. So starting at around six weeks of age, a series of vaccinations are given in order to catch the time when they will be effective while leaving as little unprotected time as possible. During this time of uncertainty, it's best not to take your pup around places where unvaccinated dogs may congregate. Some deadly viruses, such as parvovirus, can remain in the soil for six months after an infected dog has shed the virus in its feces.

So do you risk taking your possibly susceptible pup out into the big bad world full of viruses laying in wait, or do you risk isolating your impressionable pup at home with no life experiences? You make compromises. You don't take your pup to socialize in the ghetto where stray, unvaccinated dogs roam loose, or even to the dog park; instead you take him places where few other dogs frequent, and where those dogs are likely to be vaccinated and healthy. Waiting until your pup is finished with his puppy shots is like locking your child in the house until she is 8 and then expecting her to adjust. You can get around the problem of immunizations by doing a lot—although not all—of your socialization at home.

Pavlov's Dogs—and Yours

When we talk of socializing our dogs, we are really using classical conditioning to instill lifelong emotional reactions to various situations. Classical conditioning is the type of learning made famous by Pavlov and his dogs.

Pavlov's dogs are probably the most well-known dogs in the history of science. Yet for the average dog owner, the ability to drool to the sound of a bell doesn't seem to have a whole lot of practical value. After all, most people want their dogs to quit drooling! But, of course, drooling is just one of many natural reflexes that can be conditioned, and a bell is just one of many stimuli that can be used.

Classical conditioning. Here's how classically conditioning a dog to drool to a bell works: Salivating is a natural response to food in the mouth. By pairing food in the mouth with the ringing of a bell, the dog will associate the two events and in time salivate in response to just the bell ringing—just as you might salivate to a picture of a steak. Pavlov used drool in this case because it was easy to measure. However, could he have measured happiness, he would have also found that the dogs became happy when they heard the bell ring because it signaled food. In fact, Pavlov did do a lot of work with conditioning emotional responses. He mostly used fear, however, because he could measure that easily in response to shock.

Bad associations. Some fears, such as the fear of falling, are innate. You don't have to fall off a cliff to know to avoid the edge. Loud startling noises also naturally evoke fear. As a puppy ages past 12 weeks, novel objects and circumstances become more and more fear-evoking. But fears can also be learned. If you invite children over and one falls on your dog, he may develop a fear of children. He's formed an association between a child and the pain and fright of being squished. You can carry it further. If your dog now has a fear of children and the doorbell rings and children are standing there every time for a few days, he's likely to respond to the doorbell ringing by running and hiding. He's developed an association between the doorbell and the fear he feels from children, which he got from being fallen on by a child.

Had children been over many times before without falling on him, your dog would have essentially been inoculated against forming an association between children and being crushed, and he probably would not form a fearful association. This is why it's so vital to have as many guaranteed good experiences as possible before taking chances on having bad ones. The more you can control your dog's first encounters and outings, the better your chance of preventing him from forming bad associations before he's had a chance to form good or neutral ones. Think of good experiences as vaccinations against fearful associations.

Good associations. Classical conditioning also works to form good associations. When you introduce your dog to a stranger, and then give the dog a treat, you set up a positive association. Of course, you don't want your dog to end up drooling whenever he sees a stranger, so for the next encounter you might just have the stranger pet him. With each rewarding encounter, the dog forms an association between meeting a stranger and a rewarding experience. If the doorbell rings and a stranger appears, if that stranger is also associated with good things, then your dog will soon learn that the doorbell predicts good things. He will be slower to learn this association if you have already randomly rung the doorbell without anybody being there, or if you do it in between the appearance of company.

Your mission in socialization is to make sure your dog is making happy associations with as many stimuli as possible, while avoiding fearful associations—except, of course, in cases where your dog should be fearful!

Making associations. Several things help cement associations.

1. **Predictive value.** The better one stimulus predicts another, the stronger the association. The more you present one stimulus

without the other, the weaker the predictive value becomes. The farther apart in time the two stimuli are, the weaker the predictive value. For most associations, it works best to present the conditioned stimulus (the bell) a half a second before presenting the unconditioned stimulus (the food).

2. **Surprise value.** Novel stimuli and associations are learned faster than ones your dog is already accustomed to.

3. **Strong value.** High-intensity stimuli tend to make stronger associations.

4. **Innate associations.** Your dog is predisposed to make some natural associations. For example, if he gets sick to his stomach after seeing a child, he won't make the connection between nausea and children. But if he gets sick after eating a novel food, he will instantly make the association between food and illness, and will avoid eating that food in the future. That's why you should avoid feeding your nauseous dog a food, especially a new food, that you want him to continue eating. You've had this experience yourself; you eat a new food, get sick, and never want to eat it again.

Quality, not quantity. There's such a thing as too much of a good thing. Good intentions can too often lead to bad results if you overwhelm your pup. When it comes to socialization, it's the quality, not quantity, that counts. As with all things puppy, you need to introduce new experiences gradually, never pushing your pup past the point that he's scared. Fear is easy to learn but hard, if not impossible, to unlearn. It can be masked through lots of counter-conditioning, but even then it lies dormant awaiting one more event to bring it back to the surface.

Everyday Associations

Your dog's world is filled with classically conditioned associations, many inadvertent:

- What if you use your hand to slap your dog, grab him by the collar, or shake him by the scruff? Your hand becomes conditioned as an aversive stimulus. Your dog will come to flinch when he sees it coming to him.

- What if you get a new baby and hustle your dog out of the room whenever the baby comes in? The baby will come to be conditioned as an aversive stimulus.

- What if you turn off the television right before you leave your dog alone for the day? A dog that is upset when you're gone will start getting upset at the sudden silence because it's become a conditioned stimulus.
- What if your dog gets carsick when you go for a ride? The car will be conditioned as an aversive stimulus.
- What if your dog goes to the veterinary clinic for surgery? The sights and smell of the clinic will be conditioned as an aversive stimulus, which is why so many dogs pant and shake as soon as they walk into any veterinary clinic.
- What if you always feed your dog as soon as a certain television show comes on? The theme song will be conditioned as a secondary reinforcer, causing your dog to salivate just as Pavlov's did.

Child's Play

One of the first interactions you have with your baby is play. That's true whether your baby is human or canine. It's also one of the most important. Unless you play with him during these formative weeks, he will be hesitant about playing with humans. Play is one of the reasons we have dogs; it cements the human-canine bond and, perhaps more importantly, gives us a reason to act goofy.

Your puppy is used to playing with his brothers and sisters. Now who will he play with? Play is a powerful tool for making friends. It provides a safe arena in which puppies can learn new behaviors and self control. Because roles are easily reversed during play, it's an ideal situation in which to help an insecure puppy gain confidence or teach a puppy with overly competitive tendencies to cooperate.

The right games. Insecure dogs may need to start by playing cooperative rather than competitive games. Such games might include learning fun tricks, playing fetch, searching for hidden treats, or playing alongside the owner with cat toys or other toys that are easily squeaked or manipulated. These games can gradually build to more competitive games, perhaps starting with cat toys dangled on a string that can then be used for a low-key tug game.

Pushy dogs may also need to focus on cooperative games, although your rules may have to be stricter. Searching and learning games are very good for dogs that feel the need to control. If you play fetch, chasing him around for the ball he refuses to give you is probably just what he wants you to do. He needs to learn that if he doesn't bring you the ball, it means game over. Competitive games, such as tug games, should only be used if your dog has already been taught a release word. If he releases the toy on cue, he gets a treat. If he doesn't, you are in a difficult situation of either continuing the game (just what he wanted), letting go (so now he's the winner), or prying it out of his jaws (potentially not safe with an adult dog).

Educational toys. Just as many baby toys cater to parents wishing to stimulate their children's intellect as early as possible, a variety of dog toys are now available that can also stimulate your puppy. Play is an important component of learning for both puppies and children. Few things can motivate as effectively as fun and games. Don't be so preoccupied with the work of raising a puppy that you forget to have the fun. It's just as important. Maybe more.

Nice Doggy!

As soon as puppies can teeter around the whelping box, they start to make playful charges toward their littermates. At first they usually fall down before they get there, but eventually the litter looks like a drunken frat house fracas. By the time they're 6 weeks old, some puppies already seem to have established themselves as kings or queens of the litter. But their reigns tend to be short-lived. Dominance hierarchies become slightly more stable by the time the litter is 11 weeks old, and by 16 weeks long-term dominance relationships are set. Still, dominance is not an all-or-nothing thing. Just as with people, some dogs emerge as leaders in certain situations.

Dominance and you. Sometime in the midst of this jockeying, your new puppy may be coming to live with you. You may or may not have some idea of how he ranked compared to his littermates, but unless he was older, don't count on that dominant or subordinate tendency in relation to others to necessarily stick, or to translate to his relationship with people. By being very permissive and indulgent to your new puppy, you may increase his self-confidence and perhaps bolster his tendency to try to get his way. Although you may create a spoiled brat, you won't create a dog that tries to dominate you unless that dog already had those tendencies.

If your pup is at least 16 weeks old, though, he may already consider himself the cock of the walk. Such pups are more inclined to playfully tug at your clothes or bite at your hands. These are not signs that your dog is biding his time until he can take you down; mouthing and tugging are not the same as biting or attacking. Nonetheless, nobody likes being used as a human pin cushion, and biting people even in play will not be a safe adult behavior.

Because so many people have heard so many stories of how dogs are trying to dominate them so they can grow up and eat them alive, they are understandably horrified that their puppy is nipping. In most puppies nipping is totally normal and in no way indicates a devious plot or mass murderer future for your dog. Sometimes, very rarely, a puppy's biting is not in play, and knowing how to spot the signs of true aggressive biting is important.

Is It a Game or a Bite?

Many people think that if the pup is growling he must be serious. That's not true. Growling is a normal part of playing. In addition, dogs make a sound that is similar to a growl but is functionally more like human laughter. It's a rough sound made only when exhaling, and it's typical of dogs playing competitive games such as tugging games. Unfortunately many people misinterpret the sound as a growl, and even punish their dogs for it—sort of like punishing your child for laughing when playing.

That's not to say growling can't be a sign. If no play is involved and your dog starts to really growl because you've approached something he is guarding, or because you've tried to pet or groom him, or you're trying to move him, then these are inappropriate growls. Stiff body posture, lip curling, teeth bearing, and direct staring are also signs of true aggression. If they are accompanied by bites these are almost certainly not play bites, and in fact are cause for great concern.

An aggressive bite is usually quick and hard. A playful bite is more often gnawing and sequential. Playful bites tend to be gentle or exploratory rather than forceful or threatening.

Biting that occurs when the dog is afraid and hiding is usually not done in play, but in perceived self-defense. Biting that occurs when you try to do something the dog doesn't like, such as grooming or moving him, or that occurs when you get near his food, bed, or even favorite person, are probably possessiveness issues.

Real aggression is a real problem. See page 168 for some suggestions on dealing with it.

Nipping. Puppies naturally play by nipping, and without canine playmates, your pup will turn to you. Some dogs have a greater tendency to nip and mouth than others. Retrievers, bred for generations to carry things in their mouth, are "mouthy" and tend to grab and hold your hands and legs. Terriers, bred to kill small animals by biting, tend to jump and nip in excitement. Some herding breeds, bred to drive sheep and cattle by nipping at their heels, will chase and nip at running people.

When your pup bites you in play, there's no need to react violently. In fact, grabbing and slapping the pup may only convince him that you, too, are playing roughly. Chances are he will respond by playing back even more roughly. Puppies react this way to one another, escalating their fighting until the going gets so rough one cries uncle and leaves. Usually the loser comes right back for more, though, so this is not a terribly good way to discourage rough play.

If a puppy bites another pup too hard, the victim will yelp and quit playing, or sometimes yelp and retaliate. This is a valuable lesson that teaches the pup that if he bites too hard, it's game over. You can do the same. When your pup chomps down on you, yelp sharply and withdraw from him, standing still and ignoring him for twenty seconds or so. If he stops nipping and sits and behaves, quit your statue act and give him a treat. Since some dogs may find your yelp exhilarating, you may have to experiment with several versions so your dog isn't rewarded by them.

Remember, it's better to reward proper behavior than to try to squash any behavior. Don't just stop him from nipping. Reward him for not nipping by giving him a toy to carry, a ball to chase, or a chewie to gnaw. Have him sit instead and reward him.

It's important that you are not rewarding the pup for biting. Face it, half the time we people ask for it. It's fun to wriggle our fingers in front of our puppy's face, pulling them out of reach as he lunges for them. It's fun to run and squeal, and to roughhouse on the floor. In your pup's heightened state of arousal, even scolding can be exciting and rewarding. If you want him to stop nipping, ignore his behavior. Make yourself so boring he would rather play with a brick. You must also convince the rest of your family and any visitors that they must not encourage the puppy to nip.

The Little Prince

There's a reason Prince, Duke, King, and Queenie are perennial favorite dog names. The dogs didn't name themselves that. Their owners did, probably because they treated them like royalty. After all, it's fun to pamper a puppy. You can spoil him rotten and you don't have to worry you've ruined his chances of getting into college. But not so fast; spoiling your puppy can cause just as many problems as spoiling your child. It can create a brat that talks back, ignores you, and turns into a juvenile delinquent. Doting on your dog is fun, but there's a right way to do it so he doesn't actually come to think of himself as king of all he surveys.

Royalty is waited upon hand and foot, never lifting a paw to work for anything. The most important thing you can do to make sure your dog realizes you aren't the only commoner in the house is to make him work for a living. Children have chores. Your dog may not be able to set the table or take out the garbage (well, he could take the garbage out but it might not make it into the can), but he can sit for his supper. In fact, he needs to learn the satisfaction that working for his rewards can bring. Would he like a treat? OK, then he can sit for it. Would he like to go out? OK, he can stop beating on the door and ask nicely by sitting. Would he like to sleep on the bed? Only if you invite him.

Most dogs do fine with some spoiling. In fact, several studies have found no relationship exists between spoiling by the owner and subsequent aggressive behavior by the dog. Nonetheless, in dogs already predisposed to being control freaks, spoiling them by letting them call the shots may make things worse. When that happens, more drastic measures are called for (see page 168).

Learning to Learn

"You can't teach an old dog new tricks" may not be exactly true, but it's a lot harder to teach an old puppy any tricks if he hasn't already learned to learn. Any modern parent is a firm believer in educational toys and early games that introduce a baby to learning. Puppy parents should be just as big believers.

Never too young. Young puppies are still learning how to do everything. Learning to pay attention, sit, target, come, or respond to the concept of shaping or markers (you'll see what all these are in Chapter

8) will be as natural to them as learning any other new game. Some research indicates that young puppies are more receptive to reward-based training than they are at any other time in their lives. In terms of learning ability, an 8-week-old puppy's behavior and brainwave activity function at nearly adult levels. In fact, a puppy's ability to learn decreases slightly beyond the age of 16 weeks. If you wait until your pup is older for his first lessons he is more likely to be confused and intimidated by this bizarre new game you've devised. Don't put off such an important part of life by assuming your pup is too young to learn.

Stick around. One important thing you can teach your pup is to stay by you on walks. Even if you don't plan to walk your dog off-lead, dogs that have some experience off-leash are less likely to run off and become bewildered if they get loose by chance. Dogs that aren't exposed to these ideas before 12 weeks of age tend to be less likely to come when called or to stay with you on off-leash walks.

Before your pup is fast enough to outrun you, teach your pup it's to his advantage to keep an eye on you. Start by walking on-leash (see Chapter 9, page 132), making it fun and rewarding for your pup. Add some unexpected changes in direction, not to jerk him, but to give him the idea it's fun to watch you. If the area is safe, let him off-lead. Hide from him a few times and let him seek you out. If he appears to be overly interested in sniffing and wandering, sneak away and really hide. Now he knows how the game works, but in a minute or so he's going to start wishing he had paid closer attention to your whereabouts. Spy on him to make sure he's still looking but not getting too upset, and if necessary give him some clues to help him find you. When he does, give him a big reward!

Sensing the World

Now is the time to teach your puppy to use all his senses. Expose him to sights and sounds that might otherwise scare him—including that dastardly vacuum cleaner. Play music of different kinds, turning it gradually louder and louder while making it a jolly occasion, until the police finally arrive with their sirens blaring. If you do this at night, your pup will have the added benefit of experiencing flashing lights. Be sure he's already accustomed to being alone in case you have to spend the night in jail.

Teach him both voice and hand signals so he responds to either naturally. Give him practice looking at objects both near and far. Animals reared with no chance to focus on objects far away are more likely to grow up nearsighted.

Smelling. Your puppy has a great sense of smell, but many puppies need to be shown its potential. Play some scent games so he learns to use his nose as naturally as he does his other senses. Have him find some hidden treats or follow a short scent trail. Expose him to many different types of scents.

Touching. Your pup will need to let people touch him all over for the rest of his life. Look in his mouth and give him a treat. Look in his ears and give him a treat. Pick up each foot and give him a treat. Start nail clipping lessons by tipping just the very end of a nail or two at a time. Teach him the pleasure of getting a doggy massage. Too bad you can't teach him to give one.

Footing. Dogs are very touchy about their footing, and now is a good time to acclimate your pup to carpet, tile, grass, gravel, and—if you plan to show your dog—ring matting. He should also be introduced to stairs. It's easier to learn to go up stairs than it is to go down them. When going up, carry your pup to the highest step so he only has to go up one step at first. Give him a treat at the top. Then carry him to the second step from the top so he has to climb two steps. Keep on until he is starting at the bottom. What goes up must come down, so you'll need to teach him how to come down stairs the same way. Start at the next to the bottom step so he only has to do one. Then carry him up to the third to the bottom step. Continue until he's starting at the top. Of course, some puppies just tackle the stairs without any help, and extended lessons are seldom needed for most dogs.

Working. If you have special competition or working plans for your pup, now is the time to lay the foundations. The future agility competitor should start to climb low obstacles, go through small tunnels, and push through light fabric. The future search and rescue dog should be introduced to walking amidst safe rubble. He should walk over obstacles, such as ladders laid flat on the ground, that require him to learn where he places his hind legs. If weather permits, this is a good time to introduce the pup to safe, warm water, just by wading at first, but day by day venturing in farther until you are helping him swim.

Go for a Ride

With great excitement you bundle your puppy into the car for his first ride to Grandma's. By the time you arrive, your puppy has been puking like a drunken schoolgirl and giving new meaning to the phrase "projectile diarrhea." You may even have turned around to spare Grandma the shock. How did he get so bad?

The puke-mobile. Chances are your pup's car experiences have not been great so far. He may have had some rides with his breeder to the veterinarian, where he got an injection. If he wasn't carsick on the way there, chances are some of his littermates were, so he rode along in a sea of vomit and unhappiness. His next ride may have been to go home with you, an experience that was probably very frightening. Once he is nauseous and fearful in the car, it builds on itself as he comes to associate the car as a giant stimulus predicting nausea and fear.

The fun-mobile. You have to make your pup associate the car with good, not evil. That means rides to fun places—or at least, not for shots! And short rides, before nausea and diarrhea can even begin to churn. In some dogs that may mean opening the car door, setting the puppy inside, and quickly removing said puppy so he can urp and squirt on the ground. Maybe next time you can even start the engine. Gradually work up so you are driving fifty feet, then get out and take the pup for a walk. Aim for eventually driving your pup to a park where he can have fun.

Combating motion sickness. You can help some with nausea by checking on your driving habits. The more the car's speed changes, the more nauseous your riders will get. If you live in hilly country, try to maintain a constant speed up and down hills. Bring the puppy to the front of the vehicle if possible. Although a crate is usually safest, riding in a crate can increase motion sickness in many dogs. You may wish to experiment with somebody holding your pup and a lot of towels and plastic sheeting.

Finally, ask your veterinarian about motion sickness pills for your dog, which may help him feel better. Some dog owners find gingersnap cookies are helpful in alleviating carsickness—in dogs and people!

Making Friends with Animals

Many dogs grow up being uncomfortable around other dogs. Yet interacting with dogs should be an important part of your dog's social life. You have separated your puppy from the canine family he would normally have grown up with, so now you will have to find substitutes that can teach him proper canine social skills.

Family animals. If you already have another dog, you should introduce your new puppy carefully. If your current dog is at all territorial, you may need to wait until you can walk both dogs together on-leash in a neutral place. If your puppy doesn't yet know how to walk on-leash, keep the older dog on-leash but don't allow the pup to maul him. It may take a week or so for your other dog to warm up to this pesky intruder. Make sure your older dog always gets fed and petted first, and let him know he is still number one with you. Lock the pup away if need be so your older dog gets special time with you. Feed the older dog special treats when the pup comes around, so he comes to associate the puppy with good times. Place the pup in a crate and take the two for a car ride together. Your pup will naturally revere your older dog as a minor deity, and your older dog may have to give the youngster some warning growls or snaps to keep him out of his hair. Let the senior dog mildly reprimand him if he's out of hand; it's part of life's lessons. But if the puppy becomes too pesky, you may need to step in and give your older dog a break.

Introduce the family cat in a similar way, except let them meet indoors where the cat can get out of the way. The cat is more likely to have the winning edge, so you may have to crate the pup at first for his own safety.

Puppy parties. If you don't have a dog of your own, invite some friends over who have dogs you know are friendly and healthy. Bribe them by having a puppy party complete with doggy prizes. Just as you wouldn't let older children play rough with your new baby, don't let these older dogs bully your little guy. If they can't control themselves they may need to spend this first visit on-lead.

If you have no friends with dogs you may have to weigh the good and bad of venturing into dog-frequented areas. Select an area that doesn't have free-roaming dogs, and where the dogs that frequent it appear well cared for. Dog parks are too hectic to be a good idea. Find a quieter place where your dog can just meet a few other dogs. There's no need for him to get into rough-and-tumble play with them. He'll have that chance as he gets a little older. Find a puppy kindergarten class and ask their opinion about bringing your pup.

Kindergarten. Your pup's real socialization with other dogs will be on hold awaiting the completion of his puppy shots. By three to four months of age, he should be ready to meet new friends. Because 18 weeks of age marks another milestone in your pup's development, signaling the transition from puppy to adolescent, you don't have much time to squeeze in some last puppyhood experiences.

Just as your child benefits from attending a good kindergarten class, your puppy can also benefit from enrollment in a good puppy kindergarten class. A bad class can be worse than no class, however. Look for classes that emphasis reward-based training using play, toys, and treats. Run away from any class that advocates physical punishment, chain choke collars, grabbing and shaking, or alpha-rolls. Alpha-rolls are a once-popular technique in which you throw or roll the dog on his back and hold him there until he gives up or stops protesting. Remember, your puppy is not your enemy. Don't put him in a class that acts like he is. The Association of Pet Dog Trainers (www.apdt.org) may be able to suggest an instructor in your area. If you can't find one, try to get a group of friends together and have your own class.

Puppy classes are about controlled fun. Puppies should get to play with one another, but not bully each other. Puppies should get to meet all the other owners. They will do some simple training and learn that learning is fun. A good kindergarten class will have your puppy jumping with glee every time he heads there.

Friendly—or rude? Many dogs, along with their owners, have no idea about doggy etiquette. When their dogs rush up to yours, sniffing and being pushy, their owners brag about how friendly their dogs are, oblivious to the fact that your dog is frightened or indignant about a stranger taking such liberties. You wouldn't expect your child to stand still while a strange child or an adult rushed up and pushed himself on her. You need to protect your dog from such advances. Put yourself between the strange dog and yours. Ask the owner to control her dog. The dog may just be acting friendly, but he is being rude.

Meeting People

Finally, the really fun part! Your aim is to have your puppy comfortable around strangers. That doesn't mean he has to throw himself at them. After all, you wouldn't expect or want your child to rush up to every person she sees, jump in their laps, and beg for candy. Ideally your pup should be interested in strangers and approach only when invited or, better yet, only when you give permission. For that reason you don't want your pup to come to expect treats from strangers; otherwise he may be abandoning you for the Santas he sees on every corner.

Everybody wants to pat the puppy on the head, but your puppy will be much happier if they rub him under the chin or on the chest. A pat on the head is about as welcome as having an old lady pinch your cheeks if you're a kid.

It takes all kinds. Dogs don't innately understand that a person carrying a cane and wearing a heavy coat, sunglasses, hat, and high heels is not a space monster (just a fashion casualty). You can practice at home by playing dress up, letting your dog know it's you under that bizarre outfit. You'll want your puppy to meet young people, old people, men, women, people in wheelchairs, people with canes, people of all races and sizes, just about everyone but mass murderers. Well, not quite so fast. You want your puppy to meet one or two people at a time, and these people must be gentle and non-threatening.

Avoid the crowds. Don't take your puppy to a crowd with the idea of letting him meet lots of people at once. He could be stepped on, or people could start trying to reach for him to pet him all at once, and he could end up being terrified. Your puppy doesn't have to be on a campaign tour so he can meet hundreds of strangers. Meeting a few well-chosen ones under good circumstances is more valuable than meeting a horde of humans under overwhelming circumstances.

Meeting kids. If you invite the neighborhood kids over to meet the puppy, they should sit on the floor. Otherwise it's too tempting to start playing "chase the puppy" and end up frightening him. It's also too easy to drop or fall on the puppy. Children must be taught that puppies can't be handled roughly. Dogs and young children should always be supervised for both of their well-being. This is a good chance to teach the neighborhood children safe manners around dogs.

Meeting babies. You may have a more difficult time finding a baby for your puppy to meet; parents can be a little touchy about offering up their baby as training fodder for your dog. If you may one day be adding a baby to your household, however, letting your dog meet a baby while he's still a baby can be helpful. One of the most common reasons people give up the dogs they once loved is because they are now expecting a human baby. You can have both—but you should prepare.

A baby's cries may sound a lot like some of your dog's favorite toys. It's tempting to be overly protective, but trying to hide your baby from your dog or hold it overhead out of his reach is exactly what you would do if you wanted to interest your dog in a new toy (well, almost exactly; you might also throw the toy). It will only make your dog more curious, and one day he will leap up as you hold your baby so he can see what is making that squealing sound, and you'll be sure he was trying to do something dastardly, and he'll be banished to the backyard.

Instead, don't make a big deal out of hiding your baby from your dog. Let them meet through a play pen or exercise pen if you're uncomfortable. Lavish attention on your pup when the baby is in the room. Have your pup sit and then give him a treat. Continue as you move closer to the baby. Eventually your dog will come to love your baby, but no matter how much you trust your dog, don't leave him alone with a baby or small child.

Your dog may have been your baby until you brought this new hairless baby home. If you suddenly ignore your dog to dote upon the little interloper, especially if you further add to the injustice by hustling your dog out of the room just because the new darling is in there, you're setting up a recipe for a big case of jealousy. Instead, always make a fuss over the dog when the baby is around so the dog will associate the baby with good times.

Keep It Up!

Don't think that you can socialize the bejeebers out of your puppy until he's 12 weeks old and then just sit back and rest. Research in which adequately socialized prospective guide dogs were either placed in homes at 12 weeks of age or remained in the kennel (with no socialization) for at least two more weeks before going to homes showed that the group with the gap in socialization had a much higher failure rate as guide dogs. Your pup will no doubt be better socialized than these puppies were, but nonetheless, keep up some socialization even after your pup is a social butterfly.

Social maturity. Socialization and learning don't end in puppyhood. Learning is a lifelong process. After the novelty of puppyhood wears off, it's easy to put your dog's learning and activity needs on the back burner. But since many behavioral problems don't emerge until the time of social maturity at about two years of age, the more you can interact with your dog the sooner you can detect hints of problems and act on them. Far too many dogs are surrendered for behavior problems when they reach social maturity, so it is an especially critical time to maintain a good relationship with your dog.

Aging. Dogs, like many animals, naturally show age-related declines in mental function starting at about six years of age, but usually not becoming noticeable until old age. However, studies have shown that you can counteract this decline by feeding your dogs foods rich in antioxidants (with additives including Vitamins E and C, l-carnitine, and fruits and vegetables, among others) and by providing an enriched environment (consisting of social interaction, physical exercise, novel toys, and learning tasks). Each thing helps, but doing both together helps the most. The longer you provide these the better your older dog will be compared to other old dogs of a similar age. Just because your old dog is not as active as he once was is no reason to think he doesn't need stimulation.

"Man is a dog's ideal of what God should be."

—Holbrook Jackson (1874–1948)

Chapter 6
Urine Luck!

Congratulations! You are about to master the art of carpet cleaning!

But not so fast. It's possible to avoid actual mastery, although you still may have to take a few lessons. The sooner your puppy masters his housetraining lessons, the sooner you can abandon your carpet cleaning lessons. The time to start is now.

Potty-Training

Housetraining is most effectively introduced when your pup is between 7 and 9 weeks of age. Before that time, pups don't appear to be able to either grasp the idea or control themselves sufficiently. Trying to train them to do something they just can't do is going to be counterproductive. After 9 weeks of age, puppies seem to cling to whatever surface or place they were using between 7 and 9 weeks of age. So it is very important that you make sure your pup has as few chances to go in the wrong places, and as many chances to go in the right places, as possible during this crucial time.

Traditional housetraining for dogs differs from potty-training for children in one fundamental way: When potty-training children, the emphasis is on where they *should* go. When housetraining dogs, the emphasis is usually on where they *should not* go. The problem is that it's always easier to teach someone what is right rather than make them deduce it by teaching them only what is wrong. Punishing your dog for urinating in the corner may tell him that's not the right place to do it, but it leaves the entire rest of the house on the "possibly OK" list.

Potty-training, human or canine, relies on the interplay of instincts and learning. Instincts differ between the two, but learning principles are the same. In a nutshell—or in a potty—we all learn to go in a certain place because we find it rewarding to do so.

That Empty Feeling

Peeing and pooping: two of life's simple pleasures. For a puppy or a baby, emptying a full bladder or bowel is highly rewarding because it feels good—at least in comparison to holding it in.

Because the very act of relieving himself is rewarding to the puppy, he is more likely to do it again. That means pottying in a particular place increases the chance he will go there again—indoors or out. Your job is to make sure he gets rewarded for going inside as seldom as possible, and rewarded for going outside as often as possible.

Indoor rewards. If only it were that simple. The indoors is convenient and comfortable—inherently more rewarding. That's why we have indoor plumbing for us. What's more, puppies raised in indoor pens already have countless rewarding episodes of pottying indoors. Everything associated with previous rewarding experiences, including the feel of carpeting under his paws, will be conditioned to bring on the urge to potty. You need to make pottying outside so rewarding it's worth the effort to get there.

Go outside! When you potty-train a child, you wouldn't push her into the bathroom and shut the door behind her, leaving her all alone. Of course not; that would cause the child to protest, cry, and avoid the bathroom in the future. Then why would you do that with a puppy? Yet the typical dog owner pushes the pup out the door and shoves it closed behind him, leaving him all alone. The puppy protests, cries, and makes a negative association with the outdoors. The one thing he probably doesn't do is potty. Once let back inside, though, he relaxes enough to wet all over the floor—one more inside reinforcement. No matter how busy you are, early potty-training must be a family affair and social event. It must not, however, be play time. Ignore the pup's attempts to solicit play until he does his duty. Otherwise he will learn that potty time is play time, and going outside with him will be counterproductive.

Outdoor rewards. There's another reason you need to be outside. Children get praise, and sometimes treats, for their accomplishment of using the potty. Your puppy needs that, too. Keep a jar of treats by the door and grab a handful when you go outside with him. Wait until he's just finishing, then heap on the praise and give him a treat. Don't wait until you're back inside; that's too late. Remember, it's inconvenient to the puppy to go outside; you have to make the reward worth that effort.

Gotta go! Effective parent teachers are attuned to clues that their child needs to urinate or defecate, and they get the child to the potty before the child can self-reward by going elsewhere. Effective puppy teachers are equally responsive to their dog's cues and schedules.

- Immediately after a puppy awakens, he must potty.

- Within 15 minutes after eating, he must potty (did you know the act of eating puts into motion all sorts of peristaltic gut motility? It does.)

- In the middle of playing, he must potty—a lot.

- If he exercises a lot he'll drink a lot more water, and a while later he'll also have to urinate.

- If he starts whining for no reason, he has a reason, and it's going to smell bad unless you get him outside.

- When you see him sniffing and circling, he's going to go. Get him outside as fast as possible, even if you must carry him there.

- When in doubt, take him out!

On schedule. A regular schedule is important for training both children and puppies. Besides going when he awakens, after he eats, and before he goes to bed, your pup will profit from being taken out at regular intervals. A standard rule of thumb is that a puppy can hold himself for as many hours as he is months old. He can go longer, for instance, overnight, if you don't let him eat or guzzle down water before bed. That in turn means not encouraging vigorous play, which will make him thirsty, before bedtime.

You can help your puppy to have a regular bowel movement by feeding him on schedule and making sure you don't give him novel foods that may cause diarrhea.

On cue. Parents add a linking cue when they know their child is about to urinate or defecate. "Do you need to go potty?" informs the child that his actions convey information and that his feelings should be acted upon by seeking the potty. Dog owners tend not to do this, when in fact the same principles apply. In fact, once you can predict when your pup will go, you can add a cue, like "Go potty," just beforehand. By never using the cue unless you're sure he's going to eliminate, and by rewarding him each time, he will eventually learn to eliminate on cue! Or at least think about it.

Water over the Bridge

Accidents will happen. Your reaction will determine if they happen more or less. What do you do when a child has an accident? You certainly don't rub her nose in it. Rubbing your dog's nose in a mess, no matter how recently it was deposited, doesn't do anything but make him less kissable and convince him you're perverted. Nor do you whip, scold, or humiliate a child.

Such overzealous corrections when a puppy goes in the wrong place can work against your housetraining efforts in several ways. First, your dog seldom knows why you're on a rant and it causes him to distrust you. Second, your unpredictable nature causes him to be nervous, which in turn increases the likelihood he will have to urinate or defecate. Third, if he figures out that it's his pottying that gets you upset, he will avoid doing it anywhere you can see him, including outdoors. Instead, he'll wait until he can sneak into another room where he can do it safely.

Caught in the act. That doesn't mean you just ignore your dog if you catch him in the act. Give a startling "No!" or "Aght!" and scoop him up to scuttle him outside as quickly as possible. Nobody likes to be so rudely interrupted. It ruins the whole experience. Once outside, be sure to reward him when he goes in the right place.

Why shouldn't you slap him if you catch him urinating on your fine rug? Because slapping puppies often leads to hand shyness, which in turn can lead to defensive biting when startled by a hand. Slapping rarely works the first time, making it too often the first step in an escalating series of physical punishment. All you may accomplish is to teach your dog not to potty in front of you, either indoors or out.

Carpet Cleaning 101

Odors play an important role in signaling puppies and dogs to urinate or defecate. The scent of urine is like a restroom sign that encourages a dog to urinate in the same area. In fact, dogs have what's been labeled an olfactory micturition (a fancy word for urination) reflex, in which the act of sniffing urine may cause the urethral sphincter to relax, causing urination. That's why it's vitally important to clean up urine in your home. Sop up as much as you can. A wet-vacuum or a carpet cleaner is good for this. Then drench the pee spot with an odor neutralizer. Odor neutralizers, which are available from pet stores, attack the molecules that create the odors. They won't totally destroy them, but you can then have a hope of masking them with a strong scented freshener. The neutralizers only work as long as they are moist, so you can place plastic wrap over the area to keep it moist a little longer. It's impossible to cover the scent with carpet fresheners; dogs have too good a sense of smell for that.

Water, Water, Everywhere

An occasional indoor accident is almost a given, but if you're stepping in soggy spots or discovering little poop packages all around your house, then you're letting your puppy have too much unsupervised freedom. When your puppy potties in the other room, he's not being sneaky or spiteful; he's being a good little wolf and doing his potty away from his den. The problem is his den is smaller than your den.

Not in my den! Young puppies avoid eliminating in their sleeping and eating area, but they don't go far in the effort. The solution is to restrict your puppy to a dog den–sized area unless he's just relieved himself, or anytime you can't supervise. That way he'll actually make an effort to hold himself until you let him out. This keeps your floors dry, teaches him the beginnings of self-control, and increases the chance you can reward him for going outside. The modern-day equivalent of a dog den is a crate, and while your pup no doubt deserves a mansion-sized crate, that's not a good idea for housetraining. A big crate will allow your pup to stroll over to the far side and potty. If you have a large crate, put a divider in it for now. As he gets better you can gradually expand it.

Some dog housetraining advice suggests your puppy should live in a crate in order to facilitate housetraining. Perhaps if you were perched outside the crate, ready to whisk him outside every few hours, this would work. More likely, you'll miss letting him out enough, and he'll be forced to potty in his crate, both reinforcing that act and breaking down his instinctual barrier against it. More importantly, that's no life for a puppy.

Do confine your pup when you can't supervise him. Do let him out often. Once he's pottied, don't put him back in the crate. Use the time to socialize, play, snuggle and do all the fun things that make having a puppy worth all the work.

Expanding the den. Once your puppy is refraining from pottying in his den, you want to gradually enlarge the area he calls his den. Start small. Place his bed or crate in a tiny enclosed area—an area only a couple of feet beyond the boundary of his bed. Do everything you can to prevent him from soiling this area. That means being as vigilant about preventing him from soiling it as you would if it were a fine oriental rug. You are ingraining a habit: in the den, no potty; out of the den, potty. Once he goes several days without soiling his den, make it just a little bit larger. You can have his den area in the kitchen or family room so he's able to socialize with the rest of the family without having unlimited freedom. As his housetraining progresses you will be gradually expanding his den so that eventually he'll have access to an entire room, then another, and another. But that's still far in the future. Right now you're just taking it one day—and one square foot—at a time.

Escape Clauses

What if you can't take your pup out as often as needed? If you leave him in his crate or den area and force him to use it, you're training him to just give up and potty whenever he feels like it. In fact, he's rewarding himself for doing it. Instead, try to find a safe place he won't confuse with the rest of your house. A covered kennel run outside may work if the weather permits and it's absolutely escape-proof and predator-proof. Even better is an indoor/outdoor kennel, perhaps leading from a room in your house or garage to the small covered run outside. That brings us to the doggy door.

Doggy doors. One of the best housetraining tools is a doggy door. Young puppies catch on to the concept of doggy doors very quickly. You can erect a small fenced potty area outside the doggy door, and a smaller area just inside. The smaller you can make the indoor area, the more like your pup's den it will be. If possible, fill most of the area with your pup's crate, removing the door or propping it open sturdily. Now when you're gone your pup will more likely go outside to potty, practically teaching himself!

Why should he go outside? First, he should want to avoid soiling his small den area. Second, you should still be running outside with him as often as possible to reward him for pottying outside. Third, you will use odor as your secret weapon.

Odor cues. Just as you don't want the scent of urine or feces in your house, you do want it outside in the selected potty area. Keep his outdoor potty area clean, but not sterile. Dogs will tend to avoid stepping in feces when they can; otherwise, they can learn to just not care. So you should have all feces picked up. But they do need some urine scent to signal their potty area. If you have to, drag some christened newspapers or other christened substrates into the yard to seed the area with scent. If you are just bringing your puppy home from the breeder, ask if you can bring something with urine scent on it home with you. It shouldn't be hard to come by!

Newspapers and such. You may not have the doggy door option. Don't despair. There is some reasoning behind the old newspaper trick. It's not ideal, but it's better than nothing. First, spread the papers so he can't miss them. When you clean up the papers, leave one with some urine odor down. Instinct strikes again: Dogs are drawn to urinate in areas already having the scent of urine. With time he'll probably tend to use one area of the papers more than others; very often it will be the area with the urine-scented paper. Start picking up papers in areas that are never used by him until gradually the only areas of paper left are those in his preferred spot. Not too fast—you don't want him to have the pleasure of pottying on your bare floor. You want him to be rewarded by the relief of urinating or defecating on newspaper. Eventually you can move the papers outdoors and hope he follows.

There are better surfaces than newspaper. Dogs are very conscious of the substrate they use when pottying. That's why dogs raised in kennels often prefer cement or gravel—and why some dogs raised in houses seem to prefer carpeting. What sort of substrate will your dog be using? A suburban dog will probably use grass or dirt, while a city dog may use concrete or dog litter. If your goal is to have him use the grass outside, why not start with grass inside? Buy sod squares, set them on a vinyl liner, and use them as you would newspaper. When one square is soiled, take it outside and plant it. The result: a dog that prefers grass; grass outside that already smells like urine and so entices the dog; and a newly sodded lawn!

Don't forget doggy litterboxes. Yes, there is such a thing. Dog litter is made from recycled newspapers and wood pulp that is super absorbent and odor controlling. You can place it in a specially made dog litter box or make your own with a low entrance and medium-height sides.

If you have a choice, however, bypass paper-training and go straight to the outdoors or even a litterbox. It's best to get your pup using the area you expect him to use as an adult as soon as possible.

Don't Despair!

When should you start housetraining? By 5 weeks of age, puppies already tend to avoid eliminating in their sleeping area, and by 7 to 8 weeks of age they begin to have location and substrate preferences. That doesn't mean housetraining will be completed by then.

As you mop your floors yet again and your friend calls to smugly brag that her puppy is housetrained at 10 weeks of age, don't despair. Chances are your friend is either lying, terribly unobservant, or just obnoxious. True, she could have a gifted pup, but most dogs take a little longer. In fact, it's not at all uncommon for dogs of any breed to take six months or longer to learn to be even fairly housebroken. Baby girl humans are generally potty-trained before baby boy humans; the same is generally true of dogs. Toy dogs are generally harder to housetrain than large dogs.

But what if your pup never catches on? Even with children, some catch on faster than others. Simply because a child lags in toilet-training doesn't make her a hopeless case. It usually means you've tried to push too hard, go too fast, or take some shortcuts. It means you have to start all over until you find a point where your child, or puppy, is perfect—even if that means taking him out every half hour.

Physical problems. But first consider other possibilities. What if your dog can't help it? A dog that's impossible to housetrain, or an adult that reverts to soiling the house, may have a physical problem.

- Urinary tract infections cause repeated urges to urinate with little warning.

- Diabetes and kidney disease cause increased drinking along with increased urination.

- Some drugs, such as steroids, cause increased drinking and urination.

- Spayed females are more prone to urinary incontinence.

- Geriatric dogs may forget their house manners and have accidents.

- Internal parasites, gastrointestinal upsets, and some food allergies can cause uncontrollable diarrhea.

A veterinary exam is warranted in any case of housetraining failure. If a physical problem is the cause, then once the problem is cured you may still have to start all over with remedial lessons. If the problem can't be cured, you may need to make compromises with absorbent bed pads, doggy diapers, or waterproof flooring.

Involuntary emissions. You come home and bend over to greet your sweet little girl puppy, only to have her squat and urinate all over the floor! She has a classic case of submissive urination, and the best way to make it worse is to try to punish her for it. She can't help it. Submissive urination occurs in both sexes, but is more common in females than males. The good news is that she will probably outgrow it if you help her. The way to help her is to build her confidence and take care not to intimidate her. That means you avoid bending over her, staring at her, scolding her, or otherwise intimidating her. Keep your greetings calm, get down on her level, and ignore her if she urinates. By teaching her a few tricks you can increase her confidence and give her a way to earn rewards.

Some dogs just can't help dribbling urine when they're excited. They, too, will usually outgrow this excitement urination as they gain bladder control. The best treatment is to decrease the excitement level. If possible, gradually condition your dog to be calm during low excitement events, working up gradually to higher excitement events. Teach some simple low-key tricks to distract and calm him. Punishing a dog with excitement urination will only lead to confusion and possibly submissive urination.

Bad boys. Males that urinate in the house by lifting their leg on furniture or walls aren't doing it because they just have to go. They're doing it because they just have to mark. Urine marking is a natural behavior of adult dogs in which they squirt urine to claim their territory. Because it's so much a part of a mature male's behavioral repertoire, marking is hard to break. Sometimes the behavior begins when another male visits or if a female in estrus comes around. Diligent deodorizing can help, but the most effective cure is neutering. Even that's not a guarantee, especially if he's already been urine marking for a while. If he has favorite places, try feeding him or making him sleep in those areas, since dogs don't like to mark so close to their eating and sleeping quarters. Incorrigible boys can wear a belly-band inside. Think of it as a diaper for bad boys. It's a band of material that wraps around the dog's midriff. The band holds an absorbent pad in the crucial location so when the dog lifts his leg the urine is caught by the pad.

If you're having a problem with urine marking, and you're already considering neutering, make that appointment as soon as you can. Urine marking may be one of our dogs' ways of reminding us of their wolf heritage, but that doesn't mean we have to like it.

"Some days you're the dog; some days you're the hydrant."

—Unknown

Chapter 7
Just Rewards

Congratulations! You're going to learn what makes your dog tick!

Learning is about cause and effect. As we grow up, we discover that whatever we do either has no effect, pays off, or comes back to bite us in the butt. If it pays off, we're more likely to try to do the same thing again so we can get that payoff again. If it bites us in the butt we're less likely to do it again. If it has no effect, we may also be less likely to do it again because the consequence isn't worth the effort; or we may be more likely to do it again if it was fun or in some other way self-rewarding. This is the crux of learning. But you knew that. Every parent and dog owner knows that. Unfortunately, the right way to apply this knowledge is not so obvious.

Fortunately, we have a century or so of scientists, psychologists, and animal trainers who have made it their lives' work to find out how we (and our dogs) learn. How soon must a consequence follow a behavior for it to be reinforcing? How good or bad must a consequence be to affect behavior? How often or reliably must a consequence follow an action for a connection to be made? How can we get a dog to do something he's never done before? How can we get a dog to stop doing something he's already doing? And how do you do all this without the benefit of sharing the same language? By applying their findings to training your dog, you can teach yourself how to teach your dog.

What's My Motivation?

Think of your dog as an actor handed a script. The actor asks "What's my motivation?" Every time you want your dog to do something, put yourself in his paws. What's his motivation?

Motivation usually means wanting something good to happen and something bad not to happen. When we talk about something good, we're talking about reward, and when we talk about something bad, we're talking about punishment. Reward can be either adding something good (like giving a treat), or taking away something bad (like releasing a choke collar). Punishment can be either adding something bad (like tightening a choke collar) or taking away something good (like removing a bone). Technically, when you add something, whether for a reward or punishment, it's called positive reinforcement, and when you remove something, it's called negative reinforcement, but most dog trainers tend to use the term positive reinforcement to mean only rewards are used. Because of this confusion we'll try to avoid using the terms positive and negative reinforcement in this book.

Crime and Punishment

Both reward and punishment are effective and have their places. However, reward has several advantages over punishment for most of the things we want to teach our dogs (and children). One has to do with a fluke of human nature: people tend to go too far when it comes to punishment. They lose their temper, they decide to teach the dog or child a lesson he'll never forget, they take out their embarrassment for a dog's public misdeed by demonstrating their disapproval on the dog, or they figure if a little punishment didn't work, maybe more and more will until it has escalated out of control. Such cases have led to child and animal abuse, sometimes perpetrated by people who honestly thought they were doing the right thing. In fact, studies have shown that animal abuse and child abuse are linked. Don't go down that road.

Punishment problems. The other problem with punishment is that it seldom does what we want it to. It can work, but not the way we usually apply it. A child or dog that reaches up and touches a hot stove burner is punished effectively. That lesson's effectiveness relies on unique circumstances. First, it's more likely to work if it was the first time the child or dog ever touched the burner. Had they touched it at other times without pain, they might assume this was a fluke unrelated to the burner. Punishment works best when it occurs the first time you do something wrong. But when we're dealing with dogs, they've usually dug several holes, or barked a few thousand times, before we decide to do something about it. That's too late for one trial learning.

Another reason touching the hot burner worked as punishment was that it was immediate. Timing is critical when it comes to all learning, but it's especially critical when learning involves punishment. For some reason we just don't tend to make strong associations between our current actions and future bad consequences, especially if those consequences are far away. That's why procrastination is so popular. It's also why we can't seem to learn to quit eating before we're so packed we're miserable after dinner. It's as though we don't believe what we do now is really going to hurt us. It's not just people; all animals are like this. Unless punishment occurs immediately they seem to have difficulty either making the connection or really believing they could get punished again for doing the same thing.

Yet another reason the burner only has to be touched once is that the punishment is severe. If the burner were merely unpleasantly warm, the dog or child might try touching it again, especially if some reward were also associated with it. If the burner got gradually hotter, he might still tolerate it, but interestingly, it would take a higher temperature to teach him to stop touching it than it would had the burner been moderately hot to start with. This means that kind-hearted dog owners who start with a low level of punishment and then work their way up might actually end up needing a very high level of punishment before it became effective. Herein lies the quandary: If you start with too mild a punishment and work up slowly, you end up using a higher level in the long run, but if you start with a severe level you risk being too severe, and there's no way to know beforehand how much is too much or too little.

Learned helplessness. Punishment has lots of problems as a teaching tool. It can shut dogs and people down. We've all been in situations where we give up because it seems no matter what we do we just can't win or can't please our boss. If you're repeatedly punished and you can't make it stop, you give up trying to even find ways to make it stop. This phenomenon, called learned helplessness, was actually discovered using laboratory dogs that were shocked and not given a way to avoid or escape it. Unlike dogs that had been able to avoid or escape it by pressing a bar or jumping a barrier, these dogs didn't even try when they finally had the chance. They had learned that they had no control over their fate, so they just stood there and took it.

Emotional consequences. Punishment can also produce some unwanted behaviors that may be related to emotional aspects of flight or fight. Some dogs run away when faced with situations reminding them of punishment. If you're the one doing the punishing, your dog may run away when you confront him. Others strike out. Undoubtedly many dogs have been the victims of escalating punishment in which they were severely punished for guarding their food, then growled in response to punishment, then were punished for growling, then bit in response to more severe punishment, until they were labeled vicious. Severe punishment has been the advice given for years when dogs show signs of aggression, but in most cases, it's the worst way to handle it because punishment can cause aggressive behavior. Think for a second: If somebody yells at you or strikes you, does that make you feel kindly toward them? Of course not. Pain makes us strike out, and pain inflicted by somebody else makes us more likely to direct that aggression toward them.

What to do? Even at its best, punishment only tells us what not to do rather than what to do. That's fine if we're in an either-or situation. But life is seldom either-or, and the process of trial and error involved in finding out what's the right thing to do when there are so many wrong things to choose from is a recipe for learned helplessness. Sometimes we, or our dog, learn enough to suppress the behavior we've been punished for, but we don't understand the concept of what we're doing wrong. Such is the case of the dog that is punished for growling. He may eventually learn not to growl, but that doesn't mean he won't bite. A growl is a way of communicating a warning that a bite may follow; a dog that doesn't growl can still bite. He just won't give you any warning.

Wrong messages. There is a place for punishment or aversive consequences in training. Life is not just a matter of good versus nothing. The truth is that most people are so inept at training with punishment that its use should be severely curtailed. Before you resort to punishment, think what message you are sending to your dog. For example:

• Mary comes home and finds Bosco has been into the trash again, so she scolds him severely—again. What has Bosco learned? That Mary is in a bad mood when she comes home and should probably be avoided. Result: Bosco slinks away when Mary comes home.

• John finds that Bowser has urinated on the carpet. He finds Bowser sleeping, drags him to the spot, and scolds him while rubbing his nose in it. What has Bowser learned? That John doesn't like it when Bowser sleeps and that, in fact, John may be mentally unstable. Result: Bowser comes to mistrust John.

- Marsha puts a shock collar on Buffy because she keeps running at visitors threateningly. She shocks Buffy the next time Buffy runs toward a visitor. What has Buffy learned? That she was right all along; visitors do bring pain and are not to be trusted or liked. Result: Buffy challenges visitors even more.

- Jim takes Butch's food bowl away because he growled when Jim got near his bowl. What has Butch learned? That he was right; Jim did want his food, and that next time he better growl louder, or even bite to keep Jim away if Jim can't get the message. Result: Butch guards his food.

- Martha slaps Belle for growling at her other dog. What has Belle learned? That she'd better not growl even when she'd like to warn somebody she's about to bite unless they quit what they're doing. Result: Belle bites the other dog one day without warning.

- John grabs Bingo by the collar and jerks Bingo to him when Bingo finally came after John called and called. What has Bingo learned? That coming to John means punishment. Result: Bingo doesn't come at all when called.

But if these tried and untrue methods don't work, what does? Sometimes the bone works better than the stick.

Spare the Rod?

The truth is that both children and dogs do need discipline. Discipline does not specifically mean punishment. It just means requiring your child or dog to act in a civilized manner when you want them to. We've all seen obnoxious undisciplined kids whose parents can't seem to say "No." Undisciplined dogs can be just as obnoxious. Training your dog using the kindest techniques doesn't mean you never use discipline. In truth, what is kinder than teaching your child or dog to act in ways that don't cause others to flee when they see them coming? Is it kinder to banish your dog from the house because you can't teach him to behave? Is it kinder to risk your dog's life?

Battling self-rewarding behaviors. Sometimes aversive consequences do get the message across effectively. Some behaviors are so self-rewarding to the dog that nothing you can tempt him with is more rewarding. Natural or working behaviors, such as chasing, herding, hunting, and killing, are such examples. A dog that chases and kills livestock is a dog that is very likely going to be shot and killed. The chances of you convincing him that treats and praise are more rewarding than stock chasing are slim. Studies have found that the most effective way to stop stock chasing is with an electric shock collar with the shock applied just as the dog approaches the stock. Similarly, shock collars are the most effective way to teach dogs to avoid rattlesnakes. In this technique the dog is shocked when he approaches a caged rattlesnake. The dog associates the shock with the snake and usually learns to avoid snakes in one trial. This technique probably works so well because animals have an inborn ability to learn certain natural associations, such as those associated with other species. In this case a shock is a much safer way than a venomous bite to make that association.

Shock collars. Unfortunately, shock collars can now be bought easily and used by people who have no idea about association and learning. Their misuse often makes a problem worse than it does better. It also amounts to animal cruelty in many cases. A shock collar should only be used under the guidance of an experienced animal behaviorist. Before you use one, shock yourself with it so you know how it feels. People who use shock collars for regular training obviously don't know how it feels to be shocked repeatedly for insignificant things. Studies have shown that dogs trained with shock collars tend to show signs of fear during training even when the collar is removed—not exactly the bonding experience we hope training will be.

Prevention is preferable to punishment. Does that mean punishment can't be used except in extreme circumstances? Not quite. It just means extreme punishment can't be used except in extreme circumstances. If your dog has been repeatedly rewarded by raiding the garbage, the first bit of advice is to put the garbage can out of his reach. If you can't do that, and you can't watch him, you can get the point across that this is not acceptable behavior. If you catch him in the act you can make a startling noise or exclaim "No!" and unceremoniously lead him to another room for a time-out. Raiding the garbage has caused him to lose his kitchen privileges. A time-out is not a jail sentence; no matter how severe the infraction he will not spend the next week, day, or even hour mulling over the errors of his ways. After a couple of minutes any additional time is useless and simply vengeful.

Punishment works best when the dog's perception is that his own actions caused the bad consequences. That's why yelling at a dog for counter surfing is not especially effective, but setting up a tin-can pyramid on the counter that comes crashing down at his touch is. You can correct your dog from garbage exploring or counter surfing these ways, but there's an even easier way: Take out the garbage and clean off the counter. Make them unrewarding from the start.

Safe choices. If you must use aversive events to dissuade your dog, use ones that are aversive but safe. A shot of canned air blasted in the face of a dog that won't stop jumping up may help get the message across. A shot from a compressed air boat horn (held away from the dog's and your ears!) can surprise a dog and create a negative association. A shaken can filled with pennies can be startling and disruptive. Ignoring the dog briefly, stopping a game, or placing the dog in isolation (not his crate!) for two or three minutes (no longer) can also be effective.

All of us, adults, children, and dogs, experience both good and bad consequences from our behavior. As parents or dog owners we have the power to impose either, and with that power comes an awesome responsibility to temper our use of bad consequences, and when we must use punishment, to do so compassionately and fairly. You will never regret over-rewarding your dog. You will always regret over-punishing him.

Think Positive

Rewards are better at explaining to your dog what you want him to do rather than what you don't want him to do. Before you use rewards to train your dog, you have to know what your dog finds rewarding, and how your dog ranks each reward. The way to a dog's brain is not only through his stomach (although it is a major thoroughfare). For many dogs the chance to chase a ball, catch a Frisbee, or play tug is even more rewarding than a deli selection of treats. Other dogs respond to hardy petting, hearty praise, or happy partying. The strongest rewards are the chance to do the things a breed was bred to love; for example, most Greyhounds will work to chase, Border Collies to herd, and Retrievers to fetch. A ride in the car, a walk around the block, or a game in the backyard are all good rewards for a great training session. Make a list of your dog's favorite things, and remember that just because you think he ought to like it doesn't mean he likes it. He decides what's rewarding and what is not.

A fair wage. Dogs place different values on different rewards, and they know what their work is worth. They may consider a piece of kibble an equitable payment for a few feet of walking on-lead, but it's not going to cut it for the length of a football field. When you decrease the frequency of rewards you must also increase the quantity or quality of rewards. You'll need to pay your dog more for doing something he doesn't enjoy compared to the payment he'll accept for doing something he does enjoy. If your dog's behavior is slacking, it may be that he doesn't approve of the pay structure.

Don't be cheap! Something happens to people when they start giving food rewards. They become misers. They ask their dog to do complicated obedience patterns and expect them to be ecstatic over a crumb of food doled out as a reward. These are the same people who spend $20 for lunch yet insist the $1.79 dog treats must last an entire week. These are the people who spend $50 in entry fees and $200 in travel to take that same dog to an obedience trial where the dog doesn't qualify. Maybe he would have qualified if his person wasn't such a cheapskate when it came to payoffs.

Pay cuts and praise. The old school of dog training warned that if you started training your dog with treats, you would have to give your dog treats forever or he would quit working. They had a good point. If you pay your child $10 for mowing the lawn for several weeks, and then cut his pay to $5, you will end up with very long grass and an unhappy worker—even though he would be mowing blissfully had you given him $5 all along.

Nobody likes a cut in pay. And, sorry to say, most dogs consider going from treats to praise to be a big pay cut. From your dog's perspective, he's done the same job and expects the same pay. Instead of his treat, you say "What a good boy!" After a few more times your dog learns that "What a good boy!" must mean "You're not getting paid today." When you substitute praise for tangible rewards, it tells the dog he's had a pay cut. He may assume he's doing something wrong, so he may try variations, which usually don't get rewarded either. That's when most trainers say he is bored. After a while, the dog quits. Then trainers say he's stubborn. But really, he's disappointed and confused.

How can you avoid this? If you replace rewards, don't make it an either-or situation. Don't make a less-preferred reward (praise) signal a more preferred reward is off the table. Always give the less-preferred reward first, and then sometimes follow it with the more-preferred reward and sometimes not. So praise, and then give a treat—or not. Whether you're using praise, food, toys, or anything in your bag of goodies, don't ever let a less-preferred reward signal that a more-preferred reward isn't available.

But why not just give the preferred reward every time? You could. You probably should. There are, however, some reasons for not giving it every time. The way you choose to schedule rewards can have important implications about how your dog learns.

Pay Schedules

Reinforcement schedules refer to how you are paid. You behave differently depending on whether you get paid by the product or by the hour, and how dependable that pay is. Your dog is no different.

The simplest reinforcement schedule is a one-for-one exchange: You get a payoff for every correct behavior you do. When you put coins in a drink machine you receive a drink in return every time. When you first teach a dog or child to do something, you give a reward every time they do it right.

In real life, we don't get an instant reward for everything we do. Instead, much of what we do is on the basis of what scientists call fixed or variable schedules of reinforcement, either ratio, interval, or duration.

Fixed ratio. If you are only reinforced for doing a certain number of behaviors, the one-to-one ratio is lost but is replaced by a one-to-X ratio. When you reward yourself after completing 50 sit-ups, you're on a fixed ratio schedule. When you reward your child for doing 10 homework problems, she's on a fixed ratio schedule. When you reward your dog for barking five times, he's on a fixed ratio schedule.

Fixed interval. If you are only reinforced when you happen to be doing a behavior during a certain regular time period, the emphasis switches from the amount of work to the timing of work. When you know your boss checks to see if you're working every hour on the hour, then you're on a fixed interval schedule. When you check in on your child during commercial breaks to see if she's studying, she's on a fixed interval schedule. When you come home from work every day at the same time, your dog is on a fixed interval schedule.

Fixed duration. If you are only reinforced for doing something for a certain length of time, the emphasis switches to persevering. When you are paid by the hour, you're on a fixed duration schedule. When you require your child to practice piano for an hour before she can go outside, she's on a fixed duration schedule. When you require your dog to be quiet for one minute, he's on a fixed duration schedule.

The problem with fixed schedules is that they are predictable. Because of that, they tend to make behavior occur in spurts. You don't take all day to do your sit-ups; you do them all at once, usually with a fast burst at the finish. You don't work steadily throughout the day but instead save your productivity displays for the times you know the boss is coming. You don't keep working even though you're no longer on the clock. Children and dogs do the same thing. The way around this is to do away with the predictability by varying the ratio, intervals, or durations required.

Variable ratio. If instead of being reinforced for every 50 responses you are sometimes rewarded twice in a row and sometimes must wait for 100 unrewarded responses, you will be inclined to respond as fast and steadily as possible. When you play a slot machine, you are on a variable ratio schedule. When you occasionally give in to your child's incessant pleas to stay up late, she's on a variable ratio schedule. When you finally let your dog inside because he keeps hurling himself against the door while you're trying to do work, he's on a variable ratio schedule.

Variable interval. If instead of being reinforced on a regular time frame, you are sometimes reinforced close together in time and sometimes far apart in time, you will tend to work at a slow, steady rate throughout. When your boss checks in on you unpredictably throughout the day, you are on a variable interval schedule. When you check in on your child—or your dog—randomly after you put them to bed to see if they are sleeping, they're on a variable interval schedule.

Variable duration. If instead of being reinforced for doing something for a set time period you are sometimes reinforced after a short while of working and sometimes after a long while, you will tend to keep doing it for longer and longer time periods. When you hang on the phone line for the "next available operator," you are on a variable duration schedule. When your child waits at the bus stop for a bus that isn't usually close to schedule, she is on a variable duration schedule. When you let your dog out of his crate for being good for some random amount of time, he's on a variable duration schedule.

Keep on trying. These variable schedules of reinforcement have a couple of advantages. Because they are not predictable, they tend to produce more consistent behavior. You never know when the slot machine will pay off, so you keep feeding it; you never know when your boss will check on you, so you keep pretending you're working; you never know when the bus will come, so you keep waiting. But even more, variable schedules produce behavior that's more resistant to extinction; that is, they produce behavior that continues in spite of the fact that it's no longer getting reinforced for a very long time.

Think about it. When you put a coin in the soda machine you expect to get a drink. If you don't, you get angry, maybe hit it a few times, and maybe try again. If it still doesn't produce a drink, you probably assume it's out of order and you don't waste anymore money on it. When you're on a continuous schedule of reinforcement, it doesn't take long once the rewards stop before you quit. But when you're on a variable schedule of reinforcement, you may not realize the game has changed for a long time. When you put a coin in a slot machine and get nothing in return, you try again. And again. Even if the slot machine is broken and never will pay off, you keep trying, sometimes until you're broke, because you think the very next time just might be the one. Remember this: When you only reinforce a behavior sometimes, that behavior is more likely to continue for a long time even if you quit reinforcing it.

Just this once. Variable schedules also mean it can be nearly impossible to get rid of behaviors you've occasionally rewarded in the past. Parents with "just this once" in their vocabulary can thank variable schedules for cementing such behaviors as whining to stay up late or crying for candy in the checkout line. Dog owners who say "just this once" usually say it more than once, and they can thank variable schedules for their dogs barking to come inside or begging at the table. When you give in "just this once," you've placed your child or dog on a variable schedule and produced a behavior that will persist for a long time even though unrewarded. That's the downside.

Jackpot! The upside of variable schedules is that you don't have to keep giving your dog a treat every moment she's in heel position or every time she sits. You can gradually decrease the percentage of times she gets a payoff, as long as you make that payoff worthwhile. Another reason people continue to feed slot machines and buy lottery tickets even when they seldom pay off is that the payoff is out of proportion to the investment: a jackpot! So when you use a variable schedule, don't just hand out the same amount you would have handed out had you been reinforcing every time. Make it a jackpot, something worth all that work—and then some.

Variable versus continuous. Although variable schedules produce the most durable behaviors, continuous schedules tend to produce the most perfect behaviors, and to do so the fastest. Traditional obedience advice is to start by rewarding the dog every time he does something right, switching as soon as possible to rewarding him for only some of the times he does something right. But why? As we'll see later, if you start reinforcing only some behaviors and not others before the dog knows for sure what you want, won't he assume he must have done it wrong those times he doesn't get rewarded? If you were teaching your child to say "Mama," you wouldn't just praise her the first few times and then decide to only praise her for every five times she says it. Then why are we in such a hurry to only reinforce our dogs some of the time when they are learning things?

The truth is that you will get the best behavior if you reinforce every time. Are you really afraid you will run out of praise some day and she will quit responding? Is it really so hard to give some nice neck scratches or carry some small treats? Yes, it's true that behaviors on a variable schedule will continue longer in the absence of reinforcement, but how often will that really happen in your dog's everyday life? If you must switch to a variable schedule, do so only after your dog knows the behavior you want perfectly. Switching too early only makes things tough on both of you.

Working like a dog. You work for your meals. Dogs evolved working for theirs. Then why shouldn't your dog work for his? It's not as though he's slaving away at a job all day. Unemployment is a major cause of boredom in modern dogs. A few minutes, or even a half hour, of work a day in exchange for food and board is a pretty good deal.

Train your dog before his regular meal time. He will work much better for food if he is hungry! Instead of giving treats in addition to your dog's regular food, you can dole out his dinner bit by bit as rewards during training sessions. If you're in a hurry, just train for a few minutes, give a few rewards, and then give the jackpot— his entire meal.

Step by Step

How do you train a behavior that's made up of more than one step? You do it by training each component and then putting them together in a sequence, or chain. Let's use walking down steps as an example. Lots of dogs, especially puppies, have a problem learning how to go down stairs. Most people start them at the top and guide them down, perhaps rewarding them along the way or at the bottom. This works for some dogs, but not for others. The best way to teach stairs is by starting with the last step. Place the dog with his front feet on the floor and rear feet on the bottom step, and reward him when he steps down. That was easy. Now start one step higher. That was pretty easy too. Once he's mastered that, add another. With each higher step, your dog has only to learn one new step each time. When he steps down just one step, he's on the familiar ground of the steps he's already mastered. That familiar ground is itself rewarding. You do the opposite to teach going up the stairs; you start with the top steps and work down one step at a time. This process of starting at the end of a series and working backward is called back-chaining, and it can be used in a variety of situations where you can't reward your dog for every step.

Chaining for Competition

An obedience trial is a situation where chaining can work. Many dogs fail at obedience trails because they have learned that in a trial setting they don't get rewarded after each exercise (you can't carry food or toys into the ring). Most handlers try to place their dogs on variable schedules of reinforcement in hopes the dog will do all the exercises, but dogs aren't dumb. They learn a situational discrimination; that is, something about an obedience ring makes you, the human snack machine, malfunction. They may try some variations of the theme in each exercise in an effort to repair you, but that only succeeds in making the judge go wild marking minus points. Pretty soon many dogs just quit. By chaining, however, these dogs can be kept on a continuous reinforcement schedule. Here's how:

The obedience routine is usually done in the same order for most classes. First, perfect each part of the sequence. For the Novice obedience routine, perfect the heel, figure eight, stand for exam, heel off-lead, recall, and finish (the stays are a separate chain of behaviors). Once these are perfect, gradually fade out the marker but not the reward. Remember, if you need the marker to let the dog know he's doing a behavior correctly, it's too soon to chain.

Next, work with the two last behaviors of the Novice routine. The last behavior is the finish (the dog goes from facing you to heel position), and the next to last is the recall (the dog comes when called from a sit-stay). Begin by practicing the finish several times, each time followed by a jackpot reward. Once he's performing the finish eagerly, do a recall and immediately follow it with a finish and jackpot. Because the finish is now a predictor of the jackpot, the finish acts as a reward for the recall. Once your dog is reliably performing the recall and finish, then add a short off-lead heeling segment ending in a sit. The reward for the good heeling and sit is the chance to do the recall then finish—and then get the jackpot. Work backward, adding in more of the heeling sequence. After that's mastered, add the stand for exam. After that, the figure eight, and after that, the heel on lead. Each exercise rewards the previous one because it is part of a chain of reinforcers bringing the dog one step closer to the jackpot. The jackpot is always there, so he is actually on a continuous reinforcement schedule.

If he fails to do any exercise satisfactorily, the sequence ends and he either must start over or quit for the day without a jackpot. If he continues to fail exercises, you've probably chained too quickly, failed to perfect the individual exercises in the first place, provided too little incentive, or asked for too much. Even if he does succeed, don't get carried away. Doing too many long sequences can make your dog's rate of reward so low it could affect his enthusiasm.

The Power of Play

Having a dog is supposed to be fun! Don't get so caught up in training and scheduling that you forget to play with and enjoy your dog. Go on adventures, play games, take trips, party! Not only is it a reward for your dog, but for you as well.

"Show a dog a finger, and he wants the whole hand."

—Yiddish Proverb

Chapter 8
Baby Steps

Congratulations! You're going to guide your dog using logic and liver!

How do you tell your dog what you want him to do? Just as you don't teach every child using the same techniques, you don't teach every dog or every behavior using the same techniques. There's more than one way to get a dog to do something, and the way you choose depends on how big of a hurry you're in and what your long-term goals are.

What sets good trainers apart from frustrated trainers? Patience, communication skills, flexibility, and timing.

It's All in the Timing

One of your jobs as a trainer is to help your dog understand that his actions lead to your reactions in the form of rewards. And just like a good comedy skit (which is what most dog training episodes are like), it's all in the timing.

Watch any typical beginner's obedience class as the dogs learn to heel. The instructor tells the students to praise and reward their dog when the dog is in heel position. The dogs are lunging, lagging, sniffing, and jumping. One handler sees his dog in nearly heel position, says "Good dog," but by the time the word "dog" has left his lips the dog is sniffing. Another handler keeps pulling her dog back to her side, saying "Good boy," as she pulls, then the dog keeps lunging ahead as soon as she releases the leash. Yet another dog is trotting nicely by his person's side, so the person says "Good boy," then fumbles around in his pocket for a treat. Meanwhile his dog has jumped into his handler's path. These dogs aren't learning anything—or at least, not anything their handlers meant for them to learn. First, chances are they did not relate the words "Good dog" with being rewarded. Second, even if they had, they were out of position by the time their handlers finished saying it. By the time the third handler reached for a treat, his dog was well out of position. The dogs learned nothing about proper heel position because the timing and nature of the reward couldn't explain it to them.

Remember, your dog is learning that whatever he is doing at the moment he is rewarded is worth doing again. That means you can't wait to see if the instructor is watching, to clear your throat, or to find which pocket you put that treat in. You have to mark the behavior for the dog by giving him instant feedback.

It also means you have to make sure your dog is doing as few things at once as possible. At the typical obedience class, your dog is not only being exposed to this new concept of heeling, but he's swiveling his head around looking at the dog behind him, barking back at the dog that barked at him, and trying to sniff the butt of the dog in front of him. Somewhere in the middle of that he happened to meander through the correct heel position and you said "Good dog!" Now he's either more likely to repeat all those behaviors, or just the behavior that was most salient to him at the time—and chances are the heel position was at the bottom of the list. That's why you'll have much better luck training your dog away from anything that might cause him to produce a number of behaviors.

Superstitious Behaviors

Sometimes you accidentally reinforce behaviors other than the one you want. Perhaps your dog was doing two behaviors at once, such as barking at the same time he sat, and you rewarded him for sitting. Or perhaps your dog just happened to start barking at the moment you opened the door to let him in. In both cases you've reinforced barking even though you didn't plan to. Now your dog thinks you want him to bark, especially if you reward him under the same circumstances again. We say the dog's barking is a superstitious behavior, because like superstitious behaviors in people, it usually results from a coincidence that then becomes self-perpetuating. You can get rid of the superstitious behavior by using discrimination training (page 116).

Saliency

Let's talk a minute about saliency. Saliency refers to whatever is most conspicuous or noticeable. It can apply to a behavior, a reinforcement, or a cue. If you give an idea to your boss that will save the company thousands of dollars, and happen to turn it in on company stationary that you printed on pink paper, you assume the bonus you receive is for the innovative idea, not the innovative paper color. To your dog in obedience class, barking at another dog is the innovative idea, and walking in heel position is the pink paper. The more salient you can make a desired response in comparison to all the undesirable responses available, the faster your training will go.

Salient cues. Saliency also applies to cues. If you say "Sit" and at the same time you push your dog into position, do you think the dog will notice your meaningless word or your meaningful prodding more? He will notice your prodding and pushing, and that will tend to obliterate your word cue. If you had a surprising sound, instead of just another of your babbling words, then that sound might compete with the prodding. So surprise and novelty are also part of being salient.

Salient rewards. Saliency applies to reinforcements as well. Even if you've timed your "Good dog" perfectly, most of what you say to your dog blends in with all the other drivel you're constantly saying to him. A dog treat is salient. If you say "Good dog" for being in proper heel position and then hand him a treat a couple of seconds later after he's out of position, the saliency of the treat overshadows that of the praise, and his take-home message is that he was rewarded for being out of position.

Fortunately there are ways around this. You can be ready with the treat, popping it into his mouth the moment he's doing what you want. That's not as easy as it sounds, especially when you start training your dog to do things that don't happen right at your side. That's when the idea of secondary reinforcements and clickers comes in.

The Clicker Clique

We don't pop a piece of candy in our child's mouth whenever she does something right. Instead, we tell her "Good!" or maybe stick a gold star on her work. A gold star is really worthless, but it's worth a lot to a child—enough so that most children will work hard to get one. That's because the praise and the star have been linked to real rewards so that they become rewarding themselves. They've become secondary reinforcers.

Secondary reinforcers. Although the idea of secondary reinforcers has been around for decades, it took comparisons between dog and dolphin training to popularize it among dog trainers. Dolphin trainers have many challenges. Telling a dolphin "Good boy" is not inherently rewarding to a dolphin; like a dog, dolphins have no idea what that means. Dolphin trainers need to teach their pupils intricate behaviors, but they can't get a fish to the dolphin in the middle of a tank quickly enough to reward the right behaviors. So dolphin trainers have to teach the dolphins a signal that tells them "That's right!"—a sort of a gold star.

To do this they fall back on what Pavlov's dogs taught us about classical conditioning (see page 64). Pavlov found that by presenting a neutral stimulus (something the dog did not normally react to—a bell) so that it predicted an unconditioned stimulus (something the dog naturally reacted to—his dinner), the dog would eventually react to the neutral stimulus in much the same way as he did the unconditioned stimulus.

I HAVE HIM TRAINED—EVERY TIME I SIT, HE GIVES ME FOOD!

Doggy gold stars. "Good boy" is not a naturally rewarding stimulus, but you can condition it to become one. You can say "Good boy" and each time follow it with a treat. After 30, or 100, or 200 pairings, when you say "Good boy" your dog will regard it as a gold star that predicts a treat.

But remember, because you're constantly talking, human words aren't the most salient thing in your dog's surroundings. Dolphin trainers had a bigger problem: human words don't carry well under water. They solved the problem by using a whistle, a sound that has a couple of features that makes it better than human speech for both dogs and dolphins. First, it's more salient because it's not something they often hear. Second, it's more precise. It's a quick sound rather than a drawn-out "Good boy." The dog may have been doing the desired behavior on the "g" of "good," but by the time he hears the "oy" of "boy" he may be doing something entirely different. Which behavior is he being rewarded for? If you're striving for a precise behavior, a precise sound makes it clear. In dog training, we use a clicker, a cheap device that makes a distinct click sound when pressed.

Click and treat. We make the click into a secondary reinforcer by repeatedly clicking then immediately giving the dog a treat. The dog need not do anything. Again, timing is everything. The click must predict the treat. If you click but don't always follow with a treat, the click has less predictive value and may not be conditioned. If you give the treat before you click, the click has no predictive value to the dog and is not conditioned. The same is true if you give the click and the treat at the same time. If you wait too long after the click to give the treat, the dog may still make the association, but will do so at a slower rate, and at some point won't make the association at all. Ideally, you should present the treat about a half second after the click, at least at first.

Charging the clicker. When clicker trainers speak of "charging the clicker," they mean making or strengthening the association between the clicker and the unconditioned stimulus (which could be a treat, game, or even petting). To do this they repeatedly click, immediately following every click with a reward. When is it charged? Not until the dog looks at them expectantly when he hears the click.

When to skip the click. A clicker is not a magic device. Its strength lies in its ability to mark precisely those behaviors that you want to be precise. You don't always care if a behavior is precise, however. If all you want your dog to do is to go away and leave you alone for a while, using a clicker will mark only one precise moment as he walks away. This is not a job for a clicker. Instead just toss him a treat. Don't confuse the dog by making him think you're rewarding him for putting his front paw on the edge of the carpet just because you happened to click at that point. Sometimes precision is neither necessary nor good. But clicker training is the best tool for getting precise behaviors.

Clicker alternatives. A lot of people balk at clicker training simply because they want to start training today but they don't have a clicker. You don't really need a clicker to do clicker training. You can use a ballpoint pen that clicks open and shut, you can make a clucking sound with your mouth, you can use a whistle, you can even say "Good!" or if your dog is deaf, you can use a light flash or a touch. The clicker just happens to be more distinctive, but anything quick and noticeable will do as a marker. Throughout this book we will try to say "mark" instead of "click" and "marker" instead of "clicker" to accommodate the different ways you can mark a behavior.

Ways and Means

Are you ready to teach your dog to sit? Great. How will you do it? The teaching techniques of molding and luring are probably the fastest and easiest ways to teach your dog to do a single, simple behavior. If your goal is to teach your dog to sit by tomorrow, one of these methods will probably get the results you want. The problem is they won't help your dog learn to do the next behavior you want to teach. If you have long-term training goals, and perhaps a little more time to get started, consider the techniques of targeting, capturing, and shaping.

Some dogs naturally take to certain training techniques better than others. Some behaviors naturally lend themselves to certain training techniques. Be flexible in your choice of techniques, and even combine them in teaching some behaviors.

Molding. The traditional method of teaching a dog to sit is to mold him into position by pressing down on his rear and pulling up on his front. If your dog is compliant, no problem. But if he objects to being pushed and pulled, he may focus all his energy on resisting rather than concentrating on learning. In fact, because the sensation of being pushed and pulled is more salient to the dog than is your word "sit," this technique can interfere with learning a verbal cue. Another problem with molding is that the dog becomes dependent on being guided into place. Once you remove your hands it's hard for him to make the transition to doing it on his own. Although molding is not the best way to teach a dog, it is fast and it has been working for generations. You can do it. Only in some cases you can do it better.

Fading

When using aids to help position or lead your dog, you eventually have to fade them out so the dog doesn't depend on them. That step can be difficult. If you're using molding, make a movement as though you're going to touch the dog but stop short of it. If the dog has been following, he should do the behavior without your help. With time, you gradually move your hand farther from the dog. If you're using luring, you can go from holding a treat in your hand to using an empty hand and presenting the treat from your other hand. Finally, abbreviate your movements, fading them out gradually.

Luring. Instead of pushing and pulling, you can lure your dog into position. To lure your dog into a sit you would hold a treat up above and a bit behind his head, moving it down and back so he bends his knees and rocks back into a sit. Luring does away with the problems that touching brings, but it still doesn't require the dog to do much thinking. Like molding, the prompt or lure must be gradually faded.

Don't confuse luring with bribery. It's easy to fall into the bribery trap. Your dog won't come when you call, so you pull out a treat to entice him. But what have you done? You've rewarded him for not coming and taught him to wait you out until you give in and offer him a treat. If you want to offer a treat, do so before your dog is doing the wrong thing.

Targeting. What if you could teach your dog to follow a target with his nose, or touch one with his paw? You could then move the target all around to lead him into various positions. To teach "sit," you would use the target just as you used your treat, moving it up and back over the dog's head. Because the target doesn't have the treat on it, it makes it easier to fade it from training than fading the treat. If you only plan to teach your dog a couple of simple behaviors, targeting is more trouble than it's worth. Its value lies in being able to use the target for teaching many other behaviors.

Here's how to teach your dog to target. Common targets are the palm of your hand, a clear plastic lid, the end of a stick, or a piece of tape.

1. To teach your dog to target your palm with his nose, start by holding a treat between your first two fingers near their base so your dog must touch your palm to get it. As soon as he does, mark and reward.

2. As he gets the hang of it, move your hand so he has to step forward to touch it.

3. Gradually work up until he is walking several feet to touch your palm.

4. Then place the treat in your other hand so when you mark the behavior of touching, he is rewarded from the other hand. Repeat this until he is doing it reliably.

5. Then add the cue "Target!" and practice some more. Soon you can use the palm of your hand to call your dog to you and to lead him around as though with a magnet.

If you use a stick to target, you may want to attach a plastic lid to the end. Smear some peanut butter or squeeze cheese on it at first and teach your dog to target it just as you did with your palm.

Capturing. Does dog training seem like a lot of work? Would you like to do it from the comfort of your chair? Try capturing a behavior. Lock the dog in the room with you and wait until he sits, then immediately reward him. It will take a while, but eventually he will figure out that good things come to dogs who sit. And he will start sitting more and more. Then all you have to do is add a command and wait for him to sit. Only reward him when he sits on cue. OK, it's still a lot of work, and it might take a while, but you hardly had to move.

Many of the best canine movie stars are trained with a lot of captured behaviors. A dog that understands he is often rewarded for doing spontaneous behaviors will quickly not only learn to repeat rewarded behaviors, but to offer new, sometimes quirky, behaviors in hopes they, too, might be reward-worthy. A good behavior to capture is barking. But be sure you read the section of how to teach him to do it only on cue, or you may create a barking monster!

Shaping. It seems reasonable to capture naturally occurring behaviors like sitting or barking, but what about more complex ones he will never do on his own? Or what if your dog just never sits? You can shape his behavior. Shaping a behavior is like playing the children's game of "colder" and "warmer"—except you'll only use the "warmer." As your dog is learning to sit, you reward him at first for just bending his rear legs a little. Keep on doing that until he starts bending his legs reliably. Then raise your criterion and require him to bend them gradually more and more until he's sitting. A dog that understands shaping learns to modify his behavior slightly when you stop rewarding a previously rewarded behavior, and to keep modifying it until he finds what you want. That's handy for teaching and perfecting future behaviors.

Mimicry

Many anecdotal reports exist of trainers whose newest dog watched them training an older dog, and then just walked in and joined the other dog for a long sit and stay. This may be accidental, but it does seem that dogs understand the general concept of what is going on. In a controlled study, young puppies that watched their dams finding narcotics caught on faster to finding narcotics themselves than did puppies that did not watch their dams at work. But generally, dogs are better at imitating social and natural behaviors, like barking, chasing, and hunting, than they are at imitating those that require special training, such as tricks. Too bad, it sure sounded like the easy way!

The Discriminating Dog

Once you've trained your dog to perform a specific behavior consistently, you can start to train him to do it on cue. Otherwise he'll be barking or sitting every time he wants a treat, which for most dogs is pretty much all the time. You want your dog to discriminate between the times you want him to bark and the times you don't. You do this by introducing a cue: "Speak!" Only when he barks following your cue will you click and reward him. His other barks will go unmarked and unrewarded. Gradually he realizes that the only time it's worth barking is when you've said "Speak!"

Add the cue last. This training order is just reversed from the traditional dog trainer's way of teaching commands. The traditional advice is for you to say "Speak!" at the very beginning of training, while you are still trying to get the dog to bark (or sit, or heel). The problem with doing it this way is that the dog will have trial after trial of hearing the cue word but not following it with the correct behavior because he doesn't yet know the correct behavior. Is that any way to teach an association? No. You want your cue word to only be associated with the final, perfected behavior.

Non-verbal discrimination. Verbal cues aren't the only ones your dog uses for discrimination. Dogs learn face, hand, and body signals even more easily than verbal signals. They also learn situational cues fairly easily. Jumping in your lap and giving you kisses may be treatworthy in the middle of the day while you're watching television, but not at midnight when you're sound asleep. Playing mad dog and mock growling may be cute and treatworthy at home but not in public. The same is true for people; we all learn that certain behaviors are appropriate only in certain circumstances or places.

Generalization. Dogs learn discrimination surprisingly easily. What they seem to have a more difficult time with is generalization; that is, taking a behavior from one situation to another. If you've trained your dog to bark in your kitchen, and then try it out on the street, he may be hesitant at first to comply. If you've trained him to your cue, and then somebody else cues him, he may not understand it's the same cue. It may take several tries to get the idea across that the game has not changed. As dogs learn to learn, they begin to generalize more easily. That's why during training it's important to first perfect the behavior and then practice it in a variety of situations.

Stop It!

Most dog owners are more concerned with teaching their dog not to do something. "How do I teach my dog not to pull?" "How do I get him not to jump up?" They want their dog to stop: stop barking, jumping, biting, digging, begging, stealing, running away, and destroying. They go to obedience class where their dogs learn to heel, sit, lie down, stay, and come. They even learn not to pull or bark. But the dogs seldom learn how to be good household pets. They also fail to generalize what they have learned in class to places other than class or to circumstances other than on-leash practice sessions. So the obedience star comes home from graduation and as soon as his leash comes off he rips up his diploma and turns back into the household horror he always was. His obedience lessons remain just a set of tricks to be trotted out only under certain controlled conditions, but they seldom get integrated into real life.

Punishment? You can combat unwanted behaviors in several ways. Most people choose to punish an unwanted behavior. Perhaps that's why so many dogs continue to have unwanted behaviors. As you've seen (page 93), punishment has some shortcomings that make it unsuccessful in many situations. To be successful, it has to be instantaneous, consistent, strong enough but not too strong, and preferably begun before the behavior has been established. These criteria are hard to meet in most home situations.

Extinction. You may be able to extinguish a behavior by ignoring it. When a previously rewarded behavior is no longer rewarded, the dog will eventually quit doing it. How long this takes depends on the reward history. Remember the drink machine versus the slot machine examples (page 102)? If your dog has been rewarded every single time he does something but suddenly he's no longer rewarded at all, he will quit comparatively quickly. But if he has a history of being rewarded sometimes and not others, it's going to take a lot longer. If you've always rushed to the door to let your dog in when he barks, and then you suddenly quit, he will learn that not barking brings him in a lot faster than if you've occasionally let him in when he barks and then suddenly stop letting him in at all. Most dogs are only rewarded now and then for undesirable behavior, making extinguishing it all the more difficult.

Extinction burst. Extinction is made even more difficult because once you start ignoring a behavior, the dog typically goes through a phase, called an extinction burst, where he does the behavior even more than usual. In this case he'll bark like mad ("Are they deaf? Maybe they didn't hear me!"). If you wait long enough (and the police don't come), he will eventually learn that barking doesn't get him back in the house. The problem is that most owners give in during this extinction burst, flinging open the door, yelling at the dog, and grumbling for him to come inside. What has the dog learned? Persistence pays off. Superstitious behavior sometimes gets added to the mix. If the door was opened right when the dog happened to be adding to his repertoire with some howls, he's learned that you must want him to both bark and howl. So beware: If you try to extinguish a behavior but can't go through with it, you may end up with a stronger, more persistent behavior than one you started with.

Shaping bad behavior. Here's another way extinction can go awry. Let's say your dog has been jumping your fence. Fence repair is hard work, so you tack some wire on the top to make it a few inches higher. He jumps the extra few inches. So you add more. It takes some skill, but he jumps this as well. So you add a few more inches. Finally your fence looks like it surrounds a maximum security prison—and he's still getting out. You couldn't have done a better job of shaping him to be an Olympic high jumper if you were a professional coach. Sometimes learned helplessness is a good thing. Had you made the fence dauntingly high from the start, he would have given up and you would have a normal-looking fence. Don't try halfway fixes.

Discriminating good behavior. Discrimination can come to the aid when your dog is resistant to extinction. Remember that your dog can learn cues that tell him whether he may or may not be reinforced for his behavior. Moving to a new house is an ideal time to extinguish behaviors such as barking to get inside the house or escaping from the yard. The dog can learn that what worked at the old place doesn't seem to work in this new, obviously defective home. Most of us, however, can't move to a new home just to make the dog behave. We can, however, post cues that signal to our dog that his world has changed. It could be the addition of music played in the yard, or a brand-new fence—anything that reminds him that his new world doesn't work like his old one.

Incompatibility. An effective way to combat unwanted behavior is to train your dog to do an incompatible behavior. Here's where those obedience lessons pay off! For example, let's say your dog is a nuisance when company comes over because he jumps all over them. Your dog also knows how to sit. Jumping on people and sitting are two mutually exclusive behaviors. By perfecting his sit so he can sit in a variety of circumstances with a variety of distractions, including visitors, he should be able to sit on cue until you tell him he can get up. You will have to make sure he doesn't come to associate sitting with being ignored, however. The visitor should kneel down and greet the dog, and he should be handsomely rewarded for his good behavior. With practice, he will learn that sitting for greeting pays off while jumping does not.

Quick Tips

- Teach new behaviors in a quiet place away from distractions. Only when your dog knows the behavior very well should you gradually start practicing it in other places.

- Although you can train your dog off-leash when you are in a safe, enclosed area, train him on a leash when you are in an unfenced area.

- Always train in gradual steps. Give rewards for getting closer and closer to the final behavior. Be patient!

- Give a marker instantly when your dog does what you want. The faster you mark the behavior the easier it is for your dog to figure out what you like.

- Use the marker to mark a behavior, not announce a reward. Think of the marker as taking a picture of the behavior you want to show to the dog and say "Do this again!"

- Give a reward as soon as you can after the marker.

- Don't forget to praise your dog as part of the reward!

- Once your dog has learned the completed behavior and is doing it consistently, you don't have to mark it anymore. But you still need to tell him he's good and give him a reward.

- Don't start using a cue word until your dog knows the behavior.

- Just say a cue word once. Repeating it over and over won't help your dog learn it.

- Dogs learn better in short sessions. Train your dog for only about 10 to 15 minutes at a time. Always quit while he's still having fun. You can train him several times a day if you want.

- Try to end your training sessions doing something your dog can do well. You want to end on a high note!

- Don't push your dog too fast. His successes should far outweigh his failures. Just like a child, dogs like to do things they're good at.

- Every step has to be repeated many, many times—we're talking *hundreds* of times to get it right sometimes! Be patient!

- Remember, your dog didn't read the book! He will have his own way of doing things, and sometimes he will learn faster, and sometimes he will learn slower, than the book says. Let him go at his own speed.

- Your dog isn't dumb just because he can't catch on to a behavior. If he doesn't seem to get it, try a different behavior or a different way of teaching it. If he's smart enough to figure out how to find his food bowl, he's smart enough to learn a behavior. You just have to figure out how to talk to him in his language and make it worth his while.

Trial and No Error Learning

When you give rewards as consequences for doing the right thing, you're using what scientists call operant conditioning, or trial and error learning. Some people question whether the "error" part is really necessary. What if you could teach a behavior so your student almost never made mistakes while learning? You can use a technique called errorless learning in which you make it virtually impossible for the pupil to make a mistake.

Learning scent discrimination. To understand how errorless learning works, let's compare two ways of teaching your dog to identify an object with your scent on it. Traditionally, you would place one scented article among several unscented ones, and tie the unscented ones down so the dog can't lift them if he tries. The problem is that by the time the dog tries to lift a tied article, he has already chosen the wrong one and must now unlearn that choice. In other words, he has made an error.

In errorless learning, you would teach the dog to choose the scented article by presenting only that one scented article without any of the others around. Only when the dog is retrieving that scented article reliably would you add another, unscented, article, which you place so the scented article is always more enticing (for example, by throwing the scented one but not the unscented one.) If the dog starts toward the wrong article, you might redirect him toward the correct one. You would gradually add more articles and move them closer to the scented article. If you do this gradually enough the dog will continue to choose the scented article because that's the one he's always been rewarded for choosing. He doesn't have to unlearn anything, nor does he have to experience the frustration of making a mistake. Dogs and children trained with errorless learning are more excited, less frustrated, and more willing to keep working.

But everybody makes mistakes. Is this a realistic way to train? Shouldn't dogs and children have to learn that mistakes are part of life? Perhaps, but why smack them in the face with it before they have started learning what's right? Why make it so likely that the dog or child will fail? That only makes them less eager to continue learning anything. If you make it almost impossible to fail, your student will be much more eager to play the learning game. You wouldn't set your child up to fail. Then why do so many trainers set their dogs up to fail? Set your dog up to succeed!

"I've seen a look in dogs' eyes, a quickly vanishing look of amazed contempt, and I am convinced that basically dogs think humans are nuts."
— John Steinbeck (1902–1968)

Chapter 9
Home Schooling

Congratulations! You're going to train, not complain!

You know how to motivate and shape your dog. Now all you have to do is put your know-how into action. Of course, it's going to take some practice. So you might as well get started by teaching him the basics.

What Every Good Dog Should Know

No matter what your training goals are for your dog—top-notch obedience competitor, dependable working dog, or biddable companion—you will want to include the handy obedience standards of sit, down, come, heel (at least, sort of), and stay. You'll also want to address some common irritating or embarrassing misbehaviors. But first, you want to teach your dog to pay attention.

Attention! Every parent or school teacher knows the first challenge in teaching a child anything is getting her to pay attention. The same is true of teaching your dog. The traditional attention training method is to wait until your dog looks away, then say "Watch me!" and jerk the leash to get his attention. However, bullying your dog into turning his head toward you is not really what you are after. You want him to actively and willingly watch you, and to do that, you will find reward training is more effective.

Your dog naturally looks at you many times a day, so this is a perfect example of a behavior you can capture. Train in an enclosed area so you can see exactly where your dog is looking and reward him quickly.

1. When your dog looks at your face, mark the behavior instantly and reward him. He doesn't have to stare you in the eye, nor should you stare at him. Many dogs are uncomfortable with direct eye contact.

2. Repeat this until he's looking at your face reliably. This may take 20 times or 100 times.

3. Now add a distraction by holding the treat away from your body. Your dog will look at it and perhaps try to get it, but don't let him. Only when he glances back at your face should you mark and reward.

4. Work up gradually until he has to look at you for five seconds.

5. When he's doing that reliably, add the cue "Watch me!" just as he begins to turn toward you. Repeat that for more trials and then start rewarding him only when he looks to you after you have said

"Watch me!" You should still praise and pet him for looking at you without being cued; paying attention to you is always a good thing!

6. Once he is reliably watching you on cue, take him to more distracting situations and practice there. Start with minimal distractions and graduate to more distracting locales only when he is paying attention on cue. It may take a long time to get his attention in each new place, but be patient.

Your dog will have an immense advantage when he goes to obedience class or any other public place because you will always know how to get his attention.

Sit!

There's a reason that sitting is one of the first behaviors people teach their dogs. Sitting makes it almost impossible for your dog to bowl you over, plow through the door ahead of you, jump out of the car, and generally be rude and out of control. Besides, who can resist a dog who is sitting as though saying "Please?"

Because sitting is a natural behavior for dogs, it is another behavior you can capture. But for the sake of example let's use luring to teach him to sit.

1. Hold a treat just above and behind the level of his eyes. If he bends his knees and points his nose up, mark the behavior and reward him. If instead he walks backward, you can practice with his rear end a few inches from a corner to prevent him from backing up. Using a physical barrier like this technically falls in the category of molding, but that's OK. Many times we combine different techniques to train.

2. Repeat this several times, each time moving the lure further back, until finally your dog is sitting reliably upon your command.

3. Next, repeat but using only your hand without a treat to guide him. When he sits, give him a treat from your other hand.

4. Gradually abbreviate your hand movements until you are only using a small hand signal.

5. When he is sitting reliably add a verbal cue, "Sit!" right before the hand signal. The verbal signal will come to predict the hand signal, and he will soon learn to sit to both.

Please? Your dog can also learn to volunteer to sit as a means of saying "Please?" Wait until you have something your dog wants, such as a treat, and wait for him to sit. Quickly mark the behavior and reward him with whatever he wanted. After he has learned to sit for a treat he wants, generalize it to other rewards. Does he want to play ball? Rather than dropping a soggy ball in your lap, he can hold it while sitting. Does he want to go out? Rather than hurling himself at the door, he can sit politely in front of it. He will soon learn that sitting is the magic position.

Stay!

What's the use of teaching your dog to sit if he only touches his rear to the ground and then jumps back up? Technically, you don't need to teach your dog a separate "stay" command because he should remain in position until he gets the marker from you. The marker ends the behavior. Realistically, it is easier to teach your dog a cue to stay. Otherwise he may think that you are waiting for him to offer a new behavior, and may try one at the least opportune moment.

Because staying is essentially asking the dog to do nothing, we teach it in a different way than most other behaviors. For starters, we introduce the cue word as soon as we start teaching the dog to stay. That's because your dog would otherwise not know the difference between a no-reward sit and this new behavior of not moving. Second, we don't use a marker. That's because staying is an imprecise behavior that relies on duration, not action. In addition, because the marker signals the end of the behavior, the dog would be free to get up for his reward, thus creating a situation where you are rewarding the dog for getting up.

1. Cue your dog to sit. Say "Stay" and hold your palm in a "stop" signal in front of his face. Wait for a few seconds, then reward him and say "OK!"

2. If your dog is having a problem getting the concept, you can have him sit on a raised surface or behind a small barrier so it's more difficult for him to come to you.

3. Work up gradually to a longer duration. If he gets up, simply put him back in position and start over, decreasing the duration you expect of him.

4. Next, work on moving to different positions around your dog, still remaining close to him. Move in front, to either side, and behind your dog.

5. Gradually move farther away from your dog.

6. Finally introduce mild distractions, gradually working to greater ones. Remember, you want your dog to succeed! Always be sure to reward him before you give him the "OK" signal.

7. Now you are ready to work on the stay in other locations. Be sure to keep him on-lead for his safety when practicing in public areas. Eventually your dog should be steady just about anywhere.

WARNING: Dogs that are great at learning active exercises are often the hardest ones to teach to stay put!

Down!

Having a dog that will lie down quietly is a big help when you want him to stay in the room and impress your guests, if you take him to an outdoor café that allows dogs, or anytime you need him to stay out of the way. Down is another behavior that you can capture or lure. If you lure, it's easiest to start with your dog while he is sitting. Be warned, though: he may not generalize the behavior to lying down from a standing position.

1. Move the treat toward the ground. This often works better if your dog is on a raised surface so you can move the treat below the level of that surface.

2. If his elbows touch the ground, mark it and reward him. Even if he only goes partway, mark and reward just for lowering a bit. Then repeat, marking and rewarding for going down a little more and a little more. If he keeps trying to get up, you can cheat and place your hands over his shoulders to help guide (not shove!) him downward. He will catch on quickly and you can fade that hint out after only a few trials.

3. Next, repeat but without a treat in the hand you have been using to lure him. When he sits, give him a treat from your other hand.

4. Gradually abbreviate your hand movements until you are only using a small hand signal.

5. Add the verbal cue "Down" right before the hand signal.

6. Practice the down-stay just as you did the sit-stay.

Come!

Coming when called is the single most important behavior your dog can learn. Your dog probably already comes to you when he wants to play or if you have some food. Always make sure you reward him for coming, even when you haven't called him. Your real goal, however, is to have him come when called. The best time to start is when your dog is still a puppy.

1. You will need a friend to help you, and a long hallway or other enclosed area. Have your helper hold your dog while you back away, showing your dog a treat or toy.

2. The dog should be pulling and whining to get to you and the reward. Once he is, your helper should release him so he can run to you. You can even turn and run away to increase your pup's enthusiasm. Mark the moment he touches you, then quickly reward him.

3. Eventually you want to be able to touch his collar so you don't end up with a dog that dances around just outside your reach. To do that, wait until you touch or hold his collar before marking and rewarding him.

4. Once he is running to you reliably, add the cue "Come!" just before your helper releases him. Practice this several times for many sessions.

5. Once he is coming on cue, let him meander around on his own. Call "Come" and mark and reward him when he lets you touch his collar.

6. Finally, practice in lots of different places, gradually choosing places with more distractions. Keep your dog on a long light line for his safety.

Always make coming to you rewarding. If you want your dog to come so you can give him a bath or put him to bed or do anything else he doesn't really like, go get him rather than call him. Practice calling him to you during walks, giving him a reward, then letting him run free again.

Dress for Success

So far, you have been able to do much of your dog's training at home, and it made no difference what he was wearing. But as you take your training to more public places, and as he starts to walk on-leash, his outfitting starts to matter. What will he wear?

Buckle collar. A buckle collar is the traditional leather or nylon collar most dogs wear around the house. The dog's license tag should be affixed to the collar. Because this is your dog's everyday outfit, it makes sense to use it for training everyday obedience. However, a buckle collar will not give you much control if your dog lunges or pulls. A buckle collar is the training collar of choice for dogs that are already well-behaved, but is not effective for training challenges.

Choke, or slip, collar. The traditional training tool of the traditional trainer, the choke collar is not supposed to choke the dog, but to be snapped and released quickly, giving the dog a surprising and aversive sensation. Few people use a choke collar correctly, and most just end up choking and hurting the dog. In severe cases these collars can cause cervical, airway, throat, and even eye damage. It should go without saying that they should never be left on a dog when the dog is unsupervised because they can get caught on things and strangle the dog. Don't use one in the first place and you won't have that worry. You do not need or want a choke collar to train your dog using reward-based motivation.

Martingale collar. The one advantage a slip collar does have over a buckle collar is that many dogs can back out of a buckle collar, a potentially dangerous situation in public. A martingale collar is a slip collar with a limited slip, so it tightens on the dog's neck enough to be snug, but not enough to be aversive or dangerous. They are usually made of soft material. Martingales are the walking collar of choice for many breeds with small heads compared to their necks, such as Greyhounds.

Prong collar. A prong collar is a chain martingale collar with metal prongs facing toward the dog's neck. When the collar tightens, the prongs dig into the neck, usually causing the dog to stop pulling so hard. If the dog does not stop, however, the prongs have been known to become embedded in the dog's flesh. Prong collars are often suggested for dogs that are too strong for their owners to control. Some people consider them more humane than simply choking the dog, but they certainly do inflict some degree of pain, depending on the dog's fur and neck type. Most people do not use them correctly, and the dog endures a constant pressure from the prongs. Better choices are available.

Shock collar. A shock collar delivers an aversive shock from a distance. Used correctly, in the right situation, a shock collar can be effective. Used in the manner that 99% of people, including most dog trainers, use them, they can be cruel and counterproductive. Shock will make certain behaviors, such as those involving fear or aggression, worse, not better. Its use is not advised except to thwart certain self-rewarding, natural, and dangerous behaviors, such as predatory chasing, and then only under the guidance of an experienced canine behaviorist. In these cases only a very few repetitions should be necessary before the behavior is improved; if not, repeating the process seldom helps.

Harness. Harnesses are great if you are trying to teach your dog to pull. They allow your dog to maximize his power, and that's why they are used for sled dogs and weight-pulling contests. Most harnesses are not good for teaching your dog not to pull. Their primary use is for dogs with neck or throat problems that would be further damaged by collar pressure. Harnesses are also handy for small dogs that may need to be hauled up quickly to remove them from danger.

Special no-pull harnesses are available. They loop around the dog's front in such a way that when the dog pulls, the harness pulls the front legs back and hinders their forward motion, automatically slowing the dog. These harnesses are good solutions for dogs that are accomplished pullers.

Head halter. A problem with a harness or even a collar is that both are difficult tools for guiding your dog because they both guide from behind the dog's head. It's hard to lead from the rear! A head halter works on the same concept as a horse's halter does, turning the dog's head so that his body follows. The leash attaches under the dog's chin, and when pulled forward it exerts some pressure to the upper neck near the head, giving a signal similar to the type of pressure a dog would use to stop or control another dog's behavior.

It takes a little more work to accustom your dog to wearing a head halter, and it also takes practice to get used to handling your dog with one. A head halter is much more sensitive to your pulls than is a collar. If you pull a halter as hard as most people pull on a collar, you will whip your dog around by the head and risk injuring his neck. With practice, however, a head halter is the tool of choice for dogs that pull or have control issues. Its sensitivity allows weak people to walk much stronger dogs than they otherwise could. You may need to be prepared to explain the head halter to passersby, who often assume the dog is wearing a muzzle or that he is mean.

A head halter is the choice for almost any dog that has serious behavior problems. It will not prevent biting because it is not a muzzle, but it will give you better control of your dog inside the house and in public.

Leash. You will need a walking leash. It can be made of anything except chain. Chain leashes are slow to respond, hard on your hands if you have to grab them, and tend to whack your dog in the face repeatedly.

Retractable leash. The idea of a leash that extends and retracts is a good one, but such a leash should not be used in crowded places. Too many people use them to take their dog walking downtown, or to the veterinary clinic, or even a dog show, where the dog meanders around as though he were off-leash. Your dog can still trip people, start fights, and wander into traffic when on these leashes. If you drop your end, the leash tends to retract, with the heavy handle flying toward the dog, often sending the dog into a panic as the handle appears to chase him down the road. You should accustom your dog to this possibility in an enclosed space before taking the chance in the open.

Long line. A 20-foot lightweight line is handy for teaching your dog many exercises while still maintaining some control from a distance.

Playing dress up. Introduce your youngster to wearing a collar or halter by placing it on him and distracting him with treats. Take it off and then repeat the process later, keeping it on him a little longer. This time distract him with play. Make sure he associates the collar with good times.

Pockets. What about your dress? You will need a pouch or pocket for carrying treats. If you use your pocket, be careful you don't leave your clothes where your dog can find them. Dogs are notorious for chewing through pockets to vacuum up crumbs.

Leash Walking

Walking your dog should be something both of you enjoy, but too often it's an arm-stretching experience for you and a neck-snapping experience for him. Pulling is a self-perpetuating behavior. Remember, for every action there is an equal and opposite reaction. When your dog pulls forward, you pull backward. When you pull backward, your dog pulls forward. If your goal is to train for weight-pulling contests, you're doing just great. If your goal is to have a pleasant walk, you need to make it more rewarding for your dog to walk without pulling.

First steps. Leash training is often the pup's first introduction to formal training. Let's start from scratch. You need a simple buckle collar. It may feel funny to your pup at first, so he may scratch or bite at it. As soon as he stops fidgeting with it, give him a treat. Then lure him so he gets used to walking with you, still off-leash. Soon he will ignore the collar and walk with you as you dole out treats.

A new leash in life. Only now is it time to attach the leash. Traditional trainers often advocate letting the dog drag a leash for a few days, but this does nothing to make good associations with it. Instead, keep doing like you were doing before the leash was attached: encouraging your dog to walk with you while you reward him. At some point he'll decide this leash might be something he should object to, so he may freeze or flip over. Many traditional trainers think now is the time to drag him along, but that's not necessary. Just change directions and encourage him again, step by step. Take a walk to the kitchen, hand out a jackpot reward, and end the session while he still wants more. As he gets better, you can ignore him when he's tugging or dragging, being sure to mark and reward as soon as he lets the leash get slack. Gradually use your marker to say "warmer" as he gets closer and closer to heel position. He will learn that walking on your left side pays off. Once he is doing this reliably you can add the cue "walk nice." This cue tells him he just needs to be near you without pulling (you won't mark an exact position). You will work on a more formal "heel" position later.

No more pulling! So far you've been practicing walking in your yard or some place with few distractions. Of course, you want your dog to behave when walking in public, where many distractions call to him. This is when all thoughts of walking beside you evaporate, and your dog forges ahead, dragging you, his irritating human anchor, along behind.

To put a stop to this, secure your leash around your waist so you really are an anchor when your dog pulls. When he starts to pull, stop and stand in place without giving up ground or pulling back. Only when he lets the leash go slack do you mark the behavior and reward. Practice this until he stops pulling as soon as you stop.

Next, walk toward something he wants to reach. If he pulls, stop or even back up. The point is not to jerk your dog back, but to show him that pulling gets him there more slowly. When he stops pulling, go toward the goal again. The goal is his reward, but the only way he can reach it is to stop pulling!

Heel position. Most of the time we are content with a dog that just walks nicely without ripping our arm out. Sometimes, however, we want our dog to be in a more precise position, such as the heel position. You can mold a heel position by holding your dog in place with a tight lead, or you can shape it by marking and rewarding successively closer approximations to heel. A good compromise, though, is to target your dog into position.

To target with a large dog, use the palm of your hand. To target with a small dog, use a stick with a ball or plastic lid stuck to the end. See Chapter 8 to teach your dog to target.

1. Use your target to maneuver your dog into heel position. Once he is there, mark the behavior and reward him. You may not be able to get

him there at first, so at first mark and reward just for getting anywhere close. Then gradually reward him for getting closer and closer.

2. Eventually he should be in heel position and you can start to
   fade the target by closing your fist and then raising your hand
   out of position (if you are using a target on the end of a stick,
   make it gradually smaller until you just have the stick, and then
   raise the stick out of position). Be sure to continue rewarding
   him for being in the proper position.

3. Next add the cue: "Heel!"

4. After he is heeling while you walk calmly, make staying in heel
   position a game by running and turning, marking and rewarding
   when he is able to stick to your side.

Now you have a dog that walks along in heel position with his tail
wagging and eyes on you. Who could ask for more in a walking companion?

Four on the Floor

You've probably been victimized by your dog or a friend's dog as
you walked in the door and became the target of a pogo-sticking beast
jumping all over you, ruining your clothes, and nearly knocking you
over. The typical owner response is either "Oh he just loves people!" or
"Get down! I've told you a thousand times about jumping up!" as she
pulls him down. Either way, the dog got what he wanted: For just a second, he was the center of attention.

Traditional training advice is to knee the dog in the chest or to step
on his rear toes when he jumps up. These are potentially injurious to the
dog, still rewarding because he is still the center of attention, and fail to
give the dog a correct alternative behavior.

Instead, teach the dog to sit and stay instead of jumping up. Reward
him with attention, kneeling beside him for greeting. If he jumps on you,
ignore him and leave the room. He will eventually learn that the best way
to get your attention is by doing as you ask, not by demanding it.

Pay Attention to Me!

Jumping up, along with pawing at you, nudging you, barking at you,
leaning on you, mouthing you, scratching doors, or stealing objects are
often types of attention-seeking behavior. Needy, untrained, or ignored

dogs are most likely to partake in these behaviors. Most people react by attending to the dog, whether with an idle pat, an admonishment to stop it, a shove away, or even punishment. Unfortunately, even punishment is often better than nothing for these dogs, so their behavior is reinforced.

Because these dogs crave attention, you need to make sure they get it at regularly scheduled times that you choose, not the dog. Use this predictable time to train, play with, groom, or massage your dog, making him the focus of attention.

Attention-seeking behaviors should be ignored. The dog must instead learn acceptable behaviors to earn your attention. Have the dog sit and stay for your attention. If the dog is generally unruly and wants to play, you must instead wait for him to be calm before you suggest going to play. This can be difficult because most owners are so relieved the dog is finally quiet they don't want to get him riled up again. But if you want to reward your excitable dog for being calm, you must acknowledge that you don't want a dog that never does anything, but instead you want a dog that does things on your schedule.

Calm Down!

You probably said you wanted an active dog. After all, how uncool to admit you are more suited for an inactive dog. Now you have the dog of your dreams, and it's turning into a nightmare. How can you calm him down?

Chances are your dog is not hyperactive, as you are tempted to label him, but overactive for the amount of exercise you provide him. That means the solution is exercise, both mental and physical. Teach your dog tricks. Make them challenging. Capitalize on his need for stimulation and originality by capturing behaviors. More than one canine actor got its start because its owner couldn't cope with its activity and mischief level. These are the dogs that have a mind waiting to learn.

Jogging, games, and exercise can tire your dog physically, which is half (but only half) the battle. Lure coursing or weight pulling are especially strenuous workouts. Canine sports such as agility and flyball combine mental challenges with physical ones. Tracking is also a good outlet. If your dog was bred to do a job, giving him that opportunity, whether it is hunting, herding, or pulling, is one of the best ways to fulfill his needs.

Don't expect your dog to be calm without first working off some of his energy, but even then he needs to be rewarded for calm behavior. Speak calmly and quietly. Ignore his pushy or overactive behavior. Reward him for sitting or lying down and staying, and for being calm as you gently pet and massage him. Maybe he just needs to learn how good relaxing can feel.

Give!

"Keep away" can be a fun game, especially for your dog when he has something, like your underwear, that he can run around with in front of guests as you frantically chase him around the room. Each time you chase your dog with a toy or forbidden object, it rewards him because it is fun and he usually wins.

Some dogs are naturally possessive, and will not give you their treasures whether you chase them or not. They may engage in a game of tug o'war, may lie on top of the treasure, or may even growl to prevent you from taking it.

The first bit of advice is to quit competing in possession games. This can be difficult advice to follow, because these games are fun for people, too. Most dogs can continue to play these games as long as you set some ground rules. Other dogs cannot play them under any circumstances.

NOTE: If your dog is truly being aggressively possessive, growling in earnest when you try to take something from him, do not attempt the following training. The advice that follows is only for dogs that playfully or stubbornly prefer to play tug with their possessions, not for those that guard them. For advice on the latter, see page 168.

To teach a playfully possessive dog to relinquish objects on command:

1. Start with an object the dog doesn't care about, perhaps a book or cup. Place it near the dog, pick it up, return it, and reward the dog for remaining calmly in place.

2. Gradually move the object closer to the dog and repeat.

3. Gradually keep the object for longer times.

4. Replace the object with one only slightly more interesting to the dog, and repeat.

5. Again replace it with a more interesting object.

6. When he is reliably staying calmly, add a cue word: "Give!"

7. If he picks up the object, which he probably will eventually as it becomes more interesting, give the cue "Give!" and reward him for letting you take it.

8. If he does not give up the object, don't fight him for it. Just leave the room and ignore him. Game over.

9. You may have to work with a slightly less desirable object and encourage him to first take it, then drop it, before working up to a highly desirable object. Remember to always praise and reward him with something worth getting.

Shhhhhhhh...

One bark is cute. A few barks are handy. Barking every time something exciting happens is annoying. Barking to alert you to the presence of oxygen in the air is excruciating. Dogs bark for different reasons, and understanding why your dog is barking is the first step to silencing him.

Boredom barkers. Some dogs bark because they are distressed, bored, or lonely. The best remedy is to bring them inside so they can share daily activities with the rest of the family. Isolated dogs are especially prone to barking nonstop. Even moving such a dog from a pen in the far reaches of the back yard to one next to the back door can help. Better yet, give him a yard to run in. Add a doggy door so he can come inside. Give him something to do that's more fun than barking. It's hard to bark when you're busy chewing a bone or working the food out of a treat toy. And make sure he has plenty of exercise. It's hard to bark when you're asleep.

Excitement barkers. What? He's still barking sometimes? You may have an excitement barker. Squirrel in a tree? Better bark. Car on the street? Better bark. Bird in the air? Better bark. Better just bark at everything—it's hard to go wrong that way. Except in the mind of every person in earshot. If you have an excitement barker, you need to teach him that being quiet is more rewarding than barking. Wait until he is quiet momentarily and then give him a treat. This may be easier if you have him sit and stay first. Keep repeating this, gradually increasing how long he must be quiet before getting a treat. Add a cue word, such as "Shhhhh" as you start your timing. Eventually he learns that "Shhhhh" means that if he is quiet he will get a treat. Next use a variable interval reinforcement schedule (page 101); in other words, check on him randomly, and if he is being quiet when you do, give him a treat. Don't give him one if he is barking.

Don't yell at your dog to make him stop barking. He'll only think you are joining in the fun. Be calm and quiet yourself. If need be you can throw a noisy can on the ground to stop him momentarily so he can be quiet enough to begin training.

Collaring the bark. Shock collars may quell the barking momentarily, but don't work in the long term. Citronella collars, which automatically spray a distasteful citrus scent when the dog barks, are more effective, perhaps because the scent lingers. Some dogs have figured out that by barking and jumping backward they can avoid the spray; others just bark until it empties and then bark with wild abandon. Even when they do refrain from barking when the collar is on, many know it's safe to bark when the collar is off.

Some people with constant barkers prefer to surgically debark their dogs (which usually renders them with a quiet, hoarse bark), reasoning that the dog still has the pleasure of barking without causing the annoyance. This is debatable, but it is nonetheless a better alternative than relinquishing or constantly punishing the dog, as many owners do.

Your goal is not to make your dog stop barking altogether. Everybody has a need to express themselves. You just need to teach your dog when it's okay to express himself, and that there are many more rewarding things in life than barking his lungs out.

Do Fence Me In

Some misbehavior is better prevented than treated, and the best prevention is often a strong fence or leash. Dogs that chase cars, kids on bikes, or joggers in defense of their territory usually break off their chase once they have "scared" the offender away, whereas those that chase in pursuit of perceived prey usually keep after it until they catch it. You can use treatments aimed at territorial aggression (page 171) or predatory aggression (page 176), but the wise choice is to also make sure your dog is never loose in areas in which these targets could appear.

Some dogs are homebodies, but dogs of many breeds (particularly hunting breeds), intact males, and young dogs are likely to roam and explore, a practice that can result in their death. We have been told so often that "Dogs are smart" (and we know Lassie would never walk in front of a car) that we tend to ascribe survival skills to our dogs that most don't have. The truth is most dogs have no innate fear of oncoming cars. Stray dogs are also targets of shooting, poisoning, and just getting lost. Do not depend on your dog to do the wise thing and stay in your yard without a secure fence. Make that fence secure from the start so you don't inadvertently teach him how to solve fence puzzles and escape from your yard.

Hidden electric fences are seldom the best choice. Determined dogs can grit their teeth and run through, but are seldom as motivated to come back that way. Children, dognappers, and stray dogs can come into your yard and be bitten by, steal, or harass your dog.

Just because your dog has a big fenced yard doesn't mean you don't have to exercise and interact with him. Many dogs won't exercise in their own yard, and no yard can provide the human interaction your dog craves. Besides, you need the exercise!

Mounting Embarrassment

Mounting is a natural play behavior for dogs, male or female, neutered or intact. They mount each other from any direction, sometimes as a declaration of being top dog. Other dogs will be more inclined to mount when anxious. Both males and females are more likely to mount when around a female in estrus. Some dogs become overly enthusiastic and both mount and masturbate at every opportunity. They may use your leg, a pillow, a stuffed animal, or cats and dogs. This is a self-rewarding behavior, and as such is difficult to replace with other behaviors. Keeping the dog separated from favorite objects, distracting him, and enticing him to do other behaviors for rewards may help. In the case of anxiety-related mounting, anti-anxiety drugs may help.

Some dogs mount their owners as a form of control or attention-seeking behavior. These dogs may benefit from treatment for dominance-related aggression (page 178) or attention-seeking behavior (page 135). Both treatments involve ignoring unacceptable behaviors and making the dog instead earn attention from you by performing acceptable behaviors.

Don't Dig It!

Dogs dig. They dig because they are in pursuit of underground animals, such as moles, that they can hear and smell; they dig to find a warm place or a cool place to rest; they dig to escape; they dig to bury and excavate treasures; and they dig for fun. You need to know why your dog digs in order to thwart him.

If he digs in long trenches along mole tunnels, he is in hot pursuit and your best bet is to keep moles out of your yard. If he lies in his holes, he may be seeking protection from the elements. If he's hot, get him a child's wading pool. If he's cold, get him a warm shelter. If he is digging under a fence, bury wire mesh underground for several feet, going as deep as possible or bending toward the inside of the yard. If he is burying and digging up bones and treats, or if he is digging just for fun, get him his own sandbox. Salt it with bones, toys, and other fun things for him to find. Gradually bury them deeper and deeper so the game is more challenging. Make sure he is never rewarded by unearthing something outside of the box.

People have done some cruel things to their dogs in misguided efforts to cure digging. A common cruel and ineffective cure that was suggested for years was to fill any holes with water and then hold the dog's head under until he almost drowns. Of course, it didn't work. Even if it had, would a pristine yard really be worth losing your dog's trust altogether?

Don't Eat It!

He ate what? Many a dog owner has been appalled as their darling comes to lick them in the face with feces breath. What would possess such a nice dog to eat his own poop? Nobody knows, but it doesn't seem to be a nutritional deficiency or digestive disorder. It appears that eating feces may be a natural behavior for dogs, perhaps left over from their days as village waste scavengers. Why some dogs do it and others don't is a mystery. Stopping it is a challenge.

The best cure and prevention is diligent feces removal. Adding hot sauce to the feces may deter some dogs, but others just gobble it down and run for the water bowl. Commercially available food additives, usually containing monosodium glutamate, can make the feces taste bad—or at least worse—and will dissuade some dogs. Some dogs must wear a muzzle to stop the behavior, but that can be messy when they still try. Finally, in some cases the dogs appear to exhibit a compulsion to eat feces; these dogs may be helped by drugs used to treat obsessive-compulsive behavior in dogs (see page 164).

Pica. Dogs also eat other non-food objects, such as fabrics and rocks. Some of these cause obstructions and require surgical removal, so the practice is dangerous and expensive. Prevention is through diligent removal of objects from the dog's reach, possibly supplemented by drug therapy for obsessive-compulsive behavior and training that focuses on rewarding alternate behaviors. Dirt is another favorite non-food item of dogs. The reason is not understood; perhaps they have a deficiency of dirt in their diets.

Don't Fret the Small Stuff

You're not going to be able to train your dog to refrain from doing a lot of natural doggy behaviors. If your dog wants to roll in feces or carrion, it's easier to wash him off afterward or keep him on-leash than it is to fruitlessly try to stop him. If he wants to eat cat feces, horse droppings, or other such delicacies, training is not going to dissuade him. As much as we advocate training your dog to behave himself, sometimes it's just easier on everyone if you remove temptation, roll with the punches, and worry about the big stuff. We prevent the ones we can, change the ones we must, accept the ones we're left with, and love him just the same. Besides, just imagine what your dog thinks of your annoying behaviors.

"I have just three things to teach: simplicity, patience, compassion. These three are your greatest treasures." —Lao Tzu (circa 600 B.C.)

Chapter 10
Parenting Challenges

Congratulations! You've joined the majority
of people whose dogs misbehave!

Make no mistake about it. No matter how perfect your dog's parents, no matter how wonderful his puppyhood, and no matter how hard you've worked, your dog will do something you don't like. As many as 90 percent of all dog owners report some behavioral problem with their dog. If you're lucky, it will be some nuisance behavior. If you're not so lucky, it will be a more serious behavior that will disrupt his or your life. If you're smart, you will fix it.

Seek Help

The idea of going to a canine behaviorist is often met with skepticism. A doggy shrink? Will he ask about my dog's dreams? Have him analyze ink blots? Unfortunately it's fun to make fun of what is really a very serious and often life-saving specialty branch of veterinary medicine.

If your child had a behavior problem, would you rely on the advice of your neighbors? Would you put her up for adoption? No, you would seek the advice of somebody trained in the field. You would take her to a child psychologist. Then why do people with dogs with behavior problems listen to random advice, and when that doesn't work (which is no big surprise) consider relinquishment or euthanasia? Dogs with behavior problems need to see clinical canine behaviorists.

Clinical behaviorists. But what, exactly, is a clinical behaviorist? Clinical behaviorists are veterinarians who are diplomates of the American College of Veterinary Behaviorists. To become board certified, they must have extensive training and specialized experience beyond their veterinary degree, and pass a review and specialized examinations. Clinical behaviorists are trained in diagnostics and treatment, and have the advantage of being able to recognize and treat organic problems such as brain tumors, epilepsy, and chemical imbalances that may be responsible for behavior problems. They are keen observers of behavior, and may spot clues that you have either missed or misinterpreted. Your veterinarian can consult with one or refer you to one in your area (go to *www.veterinarybehaviorists.org* for a listing of diplomates).

Other sources of help. The Animal Behavior Society offers Applied Animal Behavior Certification for scientists and professionals from the fields of biology, psychology, animal science, and other related disciplines. They may have extensive training in neuroscience, learning, or animal behavior, but cannot prescribe drug treatments.

Your veterinarian may be a source of behavior information. As the field of veterinary behavioral medicine grows, more veterinarians are putting a greater emphasis on educating themselves in this area. Veterinarians are expected to keep up to date in many fields covering several species, however. They cannot be expected to be specialists in every field, and for serious behavioral problems you will be better helped by a certified clinical behaviorist. Let your veterinarian know that you are open to the idea of being referred to a specialist.

Your obedience class instructor may also be a source of information. Like veterinarians, dog trainers vary widely in their level of behavioral training. Look for a trainer who is a member of the Association of Pet Dog Trainers (*www.apdt.org*) and certified through the Certification Council for Pet Dog Trainers (*www.ccpdt.org*).

Remember, all owners who have ever trained a dog consider themselves experts. Most are not. You need to find a real expert if you want to help your dog.

Drug Therapy

Many people laugh at the idea of "Puppy Prozac" and "Doggy Downers," but just as certain drugs have made vast improvements in the quality of life for many people, so can they for many dogs. In most cases such drugs are best used in conjunction with behavioral therapy. The selection of the drug of choice will depend on the exact nature of the problem, the age and health of the dog, and often some trial and error. Only a veterinarian, preferably one who is certified in clinical behavior, is qualified to make these discriminations.

When Bad Dogs Happen to Good Owners

It's the age-old parental lament when a child does something wrong: "I blame myself." The truth is, not everything is your fault. You can be the perfect puppy parent, your dog may seem the perfect pet, but even then surprises may be in store for you when he reaches social maturity at two to three years of age. The age of social maturity is the time when aggression problems tend to emerge, for example. If the dog is innately predisposed to be aggressive, problems will emerge no matter what the dog's early experience. It's probable that good parenting skills will help lessen the severity, but they have a tough fight against genetic, hormonal, and neurochemical influences. Good parenting skills will give owners the tools to better spot and work on such problems early on, however, when they can best be addressed.

Mismatches. Sometimes it's neither the dog's nor the owner's fault, but a problem in their match. Some matches were never meant to be. Despite all the books loaded with advice on choosing a breed, people still tend to pick a breed suited for their imaginary lifestyle rather than their real one. In cases of a bad match, re-homing the dog is often the kindest solution for everyone.

The roots of behavior. The first step in choosing how to treat your dog's behavior problem is finding out what is causing it. Your dog's behaviors are the result of his inborn inclinations, his experiences, and his developmental maturity. We don't have any problem accepting that if we have two children, they have different personalities and abilities. We have no problem pointing to different life experiences to explain abilities and actions. And we have no problem accepting that our two-year-old can't learn the same things our four-year-old can.

Unfortunately, when it comes to dogs, there tends to be two kinds of explanations. The one that casual dog owners tend to subscribe to is the "bad dog" explanation. They assume behavior problems must be due to innate problems with the dog; that is, the dog is abnormal. The explanation that committed dogs owners, and often dog trainers, tend to subscribe to is the "bad management" explanation. They think all problems are the fault of poor training or rearing practices. The truth is that some problems tend to be innate, whereas others tend to be management related. Making the wrong assumption leads to improper treatment, as well as feelings of blame and guilt.

Some of the most serious behavioral problems occur in dogs that are innately abnormal. In general, severe aggression, phobias, compulsions, and separation anxiety are more likely to be largely innate. Note that innate does not mean incurable. In contrast, nuisance problems, such as disobedience, excessive barking, jumping up, and house soiling tend to be training issues. These tend to be more easily treated. Of course, both innate and experiential factors influence all these behaviors to various degrees.

Spite

One cause of unwanted behavior you should immediately discard as a possibility is spite. As far as we know, dogs do not have the capacity to plan something out of spite. Nor do dogs have the capacity to feel guilt. What owners interpret as a guilty look is almost always a worried and submissive look. Remove the words "spite" and "guilt" from your vocabulary when it comes to dog behavior.

Whines and Wherefores

When your dog has a behavior you consider a problem, first try to find out why he is doing what he's doing. Does it happen only in one situation, in one place, or at one time of day? What life experiences could be influencing his behavior? Is it really a normal canine behavior that you just consider a problem?

Dogs are dogs. Is your dog just being a dog? Dogs roll in dead stuff, chase furry animals, lick themselves in public, chew things, eat disgusting stuff, and mount each other when company is over. Punishing them for acting like dogs not only isn't going to work, but will probably produce some real behavior problems by causing the dog to fear you. Other problems stem from failures to communicate. If you can't accept dog behavior, get a kid.

Born bad? Don't forget to consider your dog's genetic heritage. Are you horrified that your greyhound chases the neighbor's cat? Are you exasperated that your terrier has moonscaped your yard in his quest for moles? These dogs are just doing what any honorable representative of their breed is supposed to do; it's you who chose that breed. Although you may be able to modify his behavior, don't expect him to ignore what his genes are screaming for him to do.

Of course, members of a breed are not clones. Each dog is an individual, and each dog has genes that cause him to deviate from the norm in various ways and extremes. Some dogs inherit genes that make them naturally shyer, more active, or more aggressive than the norm. That doesn't mean you have to accept those behaviors, but you have to understand your dog is not being obstinate when he doesn't act like other dogs of his breed. He's doing the best he can with the genes he inherited.

Acting his age? If dogs are the mental developmental equivalent of children, then puppies must be infants—just very active infants. If your puppy has the attention span of a gnat, that's normal. You wouldn't expect your two-year-old child to sit quietly through a lecture; don't expect your four-month-old puppy to pay attention through a long training session. If your puppy is chewing like a beaver, that's normal. When your baby starts to teethe, you give her something to put in her mouth. When your puppy starts to teethe, he needs something to put in his mouth, too. If your puppy is biting like a crocodile, that's normal. Children go through hitting and biting stages. We redirect them rather than punish them. The same should be true of your puppy. Don't expect your puppy to act like an adult any more than you would expect your child to act like an adult.

Bad feelings. It's hard to be good when you don't feel good. As with a child, your dog's bad behavior could be a sign of discomfort or illness.

- A dog who suddenly growls or snaps may not be misbehaving; he may be in pain. Chronic pain sources, such as ear or tooth infections, can bring on gradually increasing levels of aggression.

- Hormonal changes, especially those associated with sexual or maternal behavior, can influence fighting, roaming, urinating, and mounting.

- Hypothyroidism has been implicated in a variety of behavior disorders, including shyness, compulsive behavior, and aggression.

- Diseases such as diabetes and kidney disease, and medications such as corticosteroids, can increase thirst and urination dramatically.

- Urinary tract diseases can cause loss of housetraining skills.

- Parasites and nutritional deficiencies can cause unusual eating habits and destructive behavior.

- Sensory problems, such as deafness, can cause what appears to be disobedience.

- Brain tumors or infections can cause a variety of abnormal behavioral symptoms.

- Lead poisoning can produce neurological signs.

- Allergies can cause a dog to lick itself in ways that appear to be compulsive.

- Partial seizures can cause bouts of sudden inappropriate behavior, including aggression, compulsion, and fearfulness.

- Infectious diseases, most notably rabies, can cause aggression and other disturbances.

- Head trauma can cause brain damage, resulting in behavioral changes.

- Infectious diseases before birth can produce neurological deficits.

- Drug therapies for other conditions may have behavioral side effects.

A thorough veterinary exam, complete with bloodwork, is a good first step for any dog with behavioral problems. As with humans, some behavior problems seem to result from too much or too little of various neurotransmitters, chemical substances in the brain and nervous system that transmit neural signals. Treatment with drugs that act on these neurotransmitters can sometimes alleviate a problem or make behavior modification more effective.

A mind is a terrible thing to waste. Some behavioral problems stem from inappropriate rearing and training. The real wonder is that dogs aren't in worse mental shape than they are. Most of them are unemployed, yet have been bred to work. Most are alone, yet are naturally social animals. Most are untrained, yet are naturally inclined to learn. The biggest challenge the average dog faces is trying to make sense out of the illogical behaviors of their humans.

A major cause of delinquent behavior in young people is boredom, and dogs—especially young dogs—are no different. We routinely subject dogs to deprivations that would be criminal were they done to humans. Dogs are raised in isolated pens or kept in crates for hours or even days on end, the equivalent of solitary confinement or sensory deprivation. Dogs can't read a book, work a puzzle, play a game, or watch television when they're confined to bed; instead they often resort to chewing, barking, pacing, digging, or self-destructive behavior such as repetitive licking to one part of the body. Crating is often done in the name of training, but if the training isn't working, then the crate is really just a storage box.

Understimulation and overactivity. Dogs need mental, physical, and social stimulation. When they lack any of these they will try to make up for them any way they can. Unfortunately, confinement often creates a vicious cycle of escalating bad behavior. A dog lacking social stimulation may throw himself at his owner when he finally has the chance to inter-act, licking and jumping and making such a pest of himself in his quest for attention that his owner labels him as hyperactive and puts him back in confinement. A dog lacking physical stimulation may run helter-skelter when he finally has the chance, again prompting his owner to lock him back up. A dog lacking mental stimulation may get into all sorts of mis-chief when he finally has access to an interesting environment, causing his owner to label him destructive and put him back in the crate. This cycle of isolation and unruly behavior tends to weaken the bonding of the person to the dog, ultimately leading to the dog's relinquishment to a shelter. Crating and confinement may subdue unwanted behavior, but it won't help the dog get better.

Tell me about your childhood. It's as apt a question for dogs with behavior problems as it is for people with behavior problems. As we mentioned earlier, children have wonder years; puppies have wonder months, or even wonder weeks. Busy owners who postpone getting their puppy out to meet people and learn about the world may miss the prime socialization period, perhaps creating a dog with difficulties adjusting to certain circumstances, objects, or social situations. Puppies that experience traumatic events during puppyhood, especially between 8 and 10 weeks of age, may be left with lifelong fears. Early experiences with rough or confusing training or inescapable punishment can cause a lifelong dislike of training, reluctance to think creatively, increased emotional reactivity, and decreased ability to bond effectively. Just as with people, some dogs let traumatic events and bad upbringing roll right off. Others don't.

Puppy play. Well-intentioned owners sometimes create behavioral problems by inadvertently reinforcing or encouraging the wrong behav-iors. Cute puppy behaviors may be tolerated or rewarded, but the same behaviors may not be so cute in an adult. Play that involves biting or chasing may or may not create ongoing problems with adult play biting, playing keep-away with stolen household objects, or playing catch-me when called. Competitive games can increase a dog's confidence and readiness to stand up to a human competitor; in most dogs these do not develop into problems, but in some predisposed dogs they don't help matters. Owners can prevent some problems by controlling the situation, that is, by teaching the dog to stop tugging or running when told to. Once the dog gives up the toy or stops its behavior, the toy can be thrown and the game continued. Play is important between owner and dog, but the person should be the one to call the shots.

Just this once. The "just this once" phenomenon can set up intermittent reinforcement schedules for common nuisance behaviors such as begging, jumping up, barking to get in, or sleeping on otherwise forbidden furniture. A similar situation occurs when family members have different ideas about what is and is not permissible for the dog. Owners may inadvertently reward their dogs for unwanted behaviors; sometimes just coming out to tell the dog to stop doing what it is doing is rewarding because the dog has earned his person's presence. Indulgent owners often add to the problem by playing with, consoling, or feeding the dog on demand. Dogs that are constantly rewarded for nothing have less reason to work for rewards, and may tend to be disobedient. Dogs that are constantly coddled may become overly dependent on their owners and lack the ability to function independently. Unlike children, dogs don't have to grow up to become productive members of society, but they do need to become independent enough that they can be left alone on occasion.

Accentuate the Positive

It's not enough to ignore unwanted behavior. You have to reward wanted behavior as well—even if that behavior is just being calm. Failing to reward desirable behavior is the same as ignoring it, and a major reason that behavior modification fails or goes slowly.

If You Wanted a Stuffed Dog...

Most people who complain about their dog's behavior want the dog to stop doing this, that, or whatever. But they seldom say what they want the dog to do in its place. Decide if you want to subdue unwanted behavior or replace unwanted behavior. It's not difficult to subdue unwanted behavior. If a child is disruptive in class, put him in a time-out and the classroom is civilized. If a dog is disruptive when company comes over, lock him in his crate and the visit is peaceful. But locking away a problem doesn't fix it, because it doesn't address the cause.

A disruptive dog may be placed in time-out, perhaps put in a cage or pen. This makes the household more peaceful, but it doesn't do anything to help the dog learn appropriate behavior. Here's the problem: Anybody can do nothing. A comatose dog, a dead dog, or a stuffed dog can do nothing. But we prefer living, breathing, interactive dogs. When you focus on stopping a behavior rather than on replacing it with a better behavior, you're asking your dog to essentially play dead. And that's not usually what you want.

Trying to subdue unwanted behavior without trying to understand what causes it may give you a temporary fix, but often won't provide long-term solutions. Very few behaviors happen without reason. Often unwanted behaviors are your dog's ways of filling some need. Thwarting that behavior without redirecting it means your dog has to come up with another way to meet his needs. If you wanted a stuffed dog, you should have gotten a stuffed dog.

Redirection. Even if you don't know the cause, you can find better alternatives than having your dog do nothing. Is there a way to redirect or replace an unacceptable behavior rather than just trying to stop it? Sometimes compromises make life easier for everyone. If your dog is constantly barking to come inside and scratching to go outside, you could extinguish that behavior by ignoring it without fail. But why fight it? Just put in a doggy door and make everybody happy. Pick your battles—and then make them into peace treaties.

Getting Better

In the following two chapters we'll discuss some of the most common serious behavioral problems. We can't cover everything. Dogs are free thinkers, and yours is likely to come up with new twists of his own. In every case, first think of all the possible causes, and how all your possible treatments could be interpreted.

Remember that many problem behaviors are easier prevented than treated. Other problems are inherent in the dog's nature. Many problems may be made manageable, but comparatively few are ever completely cured. Many cases require lifelong diligence, not just a one-time treatment.

The wrong treatment can often make problems worse and more difficult to ultimately treat with the right treatment. The sooner your dog receives the appropriate treatment for his problem, the better his odds are of getting better. The most important advice of this chapter bears repeating: The best bet for receiving the appropriate diagnosis and treatment is through an applied canine behaviorist.

Will Fixing the Dog Fix the Problem?

Castrating a male dog or spaying a female dog may help with some problems. Castration is most helpful in preventing marking, interdog aggression, and some cases of dominance-related aggression. Spaying a female does not tend to have quite as many helpful behavioral effects— but it will make your life easier.

"The greatness of a Nation and its moral progress can be judged by the way its animals are treated."   —Mahatma Gandhi (1869-1948)

Chapter 11
Never Fear

Congratulations! You're going to help your dog conquer his fears!

Behaviors involving anxiety, fear, phobias, and obsessive-compulsive behavior are related neurochemically and probably share many, but not all, mechanisms. In each case, the dog overreacts to the anticipation of a perceived danger. Anxiety-related problems can be difficult to treat, especially if treatment relies solely upon training and behavior modification without accompanying drug therapy. But left untreated, they tend to get worse, often to the point that the dog damages property or himself.

Common fears are fears of strange people, strange dogs, thunder, or gun shots. Helping your dog overcome them uses similar concepts no matter what the feared object or situation.

Fears and Phobias

Dogs can be fearful for several reasons. They may be genetically predisposed, they may have been poorly socialized, or they may have had a traumatic event during a critical period. It may be difficult to know what caused your dog's fearfulness. A dog with a specific fear is more likely to be suffering the consequences of a specific event, and is the most likely to be helped through behavior modification. A dog with generalized fear is more likely to have a genetic predisposition and be the least likely to profit from training. That doesn't mean you should give up. Living in fear robs you and your dog from engaging in lots of normal fun activities, and puts your dog at risk for panic running, fear biting, and high stress levels.

Fear and control. Fears can be learned through associations with threatening or painful events. Such associations are necessary for helping dogs survive. If a dog hears a car horn, then sees an approaching car and is hit by it, if he's lucky enough to live through the ordeal he may form an association between either the oncoming car, the horn, or both and the subsequent pain. Of course, some dogs need more than one exposure before such an association dawns on them. These dogs should eventually learn to avoid the feeling of fear by moving away from the car when it approaches or blows its horn. Such dogs don't live in terror of cars because they learn how to control their situation and avoid being in the car's path. Problems arise when the dog has no such control over its environment. If the dog was forced to stand in the middle of the road with cars coming at it blowing their horns the dog would be terrified, and would probably remain terrified of cars and horns, perhaps running away at their sight or sound.

Flooding therapy. Dog owners tend to place their fearful dogs in similar situations of no control. If a dog is afraid of people, traditional advice is to take the dog to a shopping center and have as many people as possible pet him, holding the dog in place if necessary. This is akin to staking the dog that was hit by a car in the middle of the highway. The dog has no control over his own well-being, and having no control increases his anxiety and fear. In fact, some dogs, having unsuccessfully tried to escape, turn to the only control left to them: growling or biting in self-defense. The horrified owner then typically punishes the dog and sometimes even decides he can't be trusted and gives him up.

This practice of flooding the dog with whatever it is he is afraid of while preventing him from escaping typically doesn't work for a couple of reasons. First is the dog's lack of control over the situation. Dogs with a history of being able to exert control over their own lives tend to be more confident and more resistant to fear than dogs without such a history. Unfortunately dog owners have been taught to remove as much control from their dogs as possible, for example, by ignoring them when they whine or bark to get out of a crate. Dogs can be given control by rewarding them for good behaviors that they initiate, for example, by letting them out of the crate for being quiet for one minute.

Second, flooding (as this procedure is known) depends on the dog becoming so habituated to the fearful stimulus that he can no longer maintain his level of fearfulness. Most people don't wait that long. They go to the shopping center for an hour of petting (or tormenting, in the dog's view), and while the dog eventually may give up his attempts to escape, his fear probably has not diminished appreciably. He leaves the shopping center having learned that he can't escape from these people who seem to have an unnatural interest in him, his owner won't help him, and being at the shopping center is a very scary place to be. When his owner takes him back the following week for round two, he's even more scared. If you remove the dog from the situation before his fear has subsided, you're likely to make it worse. If you continue to flood him for short periods in which his fear never subsides, you're likely to make it even worse. Unless you plan to get a tent and live in the shopping center parking lot for a week or more, this probably isn't the ideal way for you to cope with a shy dog. Think of it this way: If your child were afraid of heights, how effective do you think it would be if you strapped her into a harness and dangled her from a rooftop for an hour at a time once a week? (Hint: not very.)

Gradual desensitization. Most people would prefer to try other means, although the going is often painfully slow. If we consider that a training session isn't successful unless it ends with the dog in a relatively non-fearful state, then we're either going to have to have marathon sessions or less frightening situations. Rather than starting by dangling your child off the twentieth story, wouldn't it be better to start by having her look out the second story window? Rather than starting by taking your dog to a parade, wouldn't it be better to start by taking him on a walk with one other person?

Fearful children are best helped by confidence-building exercises that help them become competent in the area they fear. A child who fears public speaking won't be helped by thrusting her unprepared in front of a crowd; instead, she will be helped by practicing saying just a few lines in front of a friend or two, gradually working up to more lines and more people only when she is competent at easier levels. Effective teachers also add rewards to the situation. Instead of ridiculing the child for being afraid, the child is praised and rewarded for completing each simple task.

Fearful dogs can be helped the same way. You need to help your dog build his confidence and feeling of control in such a way that at the end of each session he is not fearful. You do this by combining several behavioral techniques.

1. **Response prevention.** Although you want to teach your dog to have some control, you don't want him to learn that his control is through escape or biting. If you let him run away, all he learns is to run away again. Instead, give him some way of earning his way to a point farther from the stimulus. For example, if he does a trick, you can then take him for a walk away from people for a minute. Better, if he allows a person to approach or touch him, he is rewarded by getting to then move away.

2. **Gradual desensitization.** Your goal is to start each session at a level that may cause some anxiety to your dog, but not so much that the dog is still fearful at that level at the end of the session.

That may mean that instead of walking on the shopping center sidewalks, you just walk around the perimeter the first day. Only advance one step closer when your dog is at ease at the previous level. Remember, your dog is learning to be calm. If he's still afraid at the end of a session, all you have taught him is how to be scared.

3. **Counter-conditioning.** It's easy for your dog to be fearful when he has nothing else to do but stand there and focus on the object of his fear. But if you can get him to do something incompatible with fear, such as relaxing, eating, playing, hunting, or walking, the dog will associate good things and good feelings with the feared object. This is one reason taking your dog for a walk, or hunting, with another person is more helpful than meeting a stranger at a shopping center. You can have somebody visit while you massage your dog, or feed him in the presence of strangers.

4. **Imitation.** Your dog won't be helped if he sees other dogs acting fearful, but he might be encouraged to join in if his best doggy friend is getting petted and eating treats from somebody else. Imitation won't help a lot, but it can help push a dog one way or the other. Don't forget that your dog can cue off of you as well. Don't clutch him to you, pull on the leash, or coddle him when he acts fearful. Instead, if something startling happens, act as though it's funny; if a stranger appears, act jolly.

Putting these together, you can come up with a training plan in which you will very gradually expose your dog to strangers, having your dog do something incompatible with being fearful, and asking your dog to do some simple tricks in exchange for food or play rewards.

"All dogs like me!" It may take a while before your dog even gets to the point of meeting strangers. When you do, you must avoid the people who proclaim "All dogs like me!" and then insist on being the special one who will single-handedly bring your dog around. These people tend to overwhelm shy dogs and never listen to you when you say that's enough.

In fact, a big part of the problem of socializing a shy dog is that people are social morons to most dogs. They approach head on, look the dog in the eye, reach out to put a hand on top of the dog's head, and maybe even add a chest thumping, a hug, or a face to face encounter— every one of which screams out to the dog as a social threat in dog language! This is one case where thinking of dogs as kids goes seriously wrong. Dogs are hardwired to respond to body language in dog terms, and polite dogs do none of the above. The problem is that it is virtually impossible to convince a person not to do these things!

Impolite dogs rush up to strangers head on, staring them in the eye. If they are especially domineering, they may place a paw on the other's shoulder (just as we might pet the dog) or even try to mount (just as we might hug the dog). Now your dog's worst fears have been realized; he just knew strangers were out to get him.

Polite dogs greet each other by stopping a short distance away and standing sideways rather than straight on toward the dog they are meeting. They avoid direct eye contact. They wait for the other dog to make some movement of approach. That's what people should do when meeting your dog. If your dog doesn't move toward them, that's as close as they get. If he does, and indicates he would accept petting, they should pet him under the chin or on the forechest. Dogs actually like that.

Attention. Like shy children, dogs seem more afraid of the attention of a stranger than they are of the presence of a stranger. Have the stranger stand with her back to your dog so your dog can be the one to approach and sniff. The stranger shouldn't talk to or reach for the dog. Only gradually should you get to the point where the person touches the dog first. During this time your dog may be confused about what to do. Remember, he needs the confidence of knowing he is doing the right thing, so now is a good time to reward him for doing some simple tricks. Often a dog told to sit and stay will tolerate the approach of a stranger better than one given no directions.

What if your dog can never seem to get to the point where he can be without fear, even at the lowest of exposure levels? Then you can no longer postpone consulting a canine behaviorist trained in the use of antianxiety or even antidepressant drugs, both of which can help your dog experience being calm in otherwise fear-evoking situations. Drugs don't take the place of training, but they can greatly help alongside of it.

Worth a Try?

A couple of new aids have been introduced on the market that may help dogs feel somewhat calmer. Dog-appeasing pheromones, which mimic the scent of a lactating female, may have a calming effect to dogs that inhale them. They can be sprayed around an area, or automatically dispensed periodically. Another relatively new aid is the antianxiety wrap, an elasticized body wrap that appears to make some dogs feel more secure. Just don't let him rip it up while you're gone!

Don't Leave Me!

Separation distress is a normal behavior of young dogs and wolves. Under natural circumstances, separation from the dam and littermates would be a gradual process, allowing the youngster to adjust, often with the opportunity to scamper back to safety when things got too scary. In domestic dogs, it's more often an abrupt process. The pup may experience its first separation only when it goes to its new home. Even there, his doting new owner may tend to spend all her time with him, but then abruptly leave him for long periods. When separated from the base of support, both dogs and children have lowered thresholds for fear, so they are more likely to be scared by adverse happenings when all alone. At this point fearful behavior can overlay distressed behavior. The dog can then associate being alone with being fearful, and the situation builds on itself.

Spoiling? People who have dogs with separation anxiety are often accused of fostering the condition by spoiling the dog, becoming too close to the dog, or allowing the dog to be overly dependent upon them.

This does not seem to be the case, however. Many spoiled, dependent dogs have no problem being left alone. It's more likely that certain dogs are born with a predisposition toward separation anxiety or anxiety in general, and these dogs may be more likely to manifest the problem depending on their early separation experiences.

Some evidence exists to suggest that separation anxiety appears to be related to panic attacks, in this case triggered by separation. Children who suffer from separation anxiety have a greater chance of suffering from panic attacks as adults.

Signs. So how do you know your dog has a problem? The first sign may be coming home and gasping as you realize you've been vandalized. Then you realize your vandal must have chewed and dug and used your floor for a bathroom. This is no ordinary vandal. It's your dog in panic mode. And while your first instinct is to kill him, or at least severely maim and terrorize him, that won't help one bit.

The nature and timing of the damage leads many owners to assume their dog is spiting them for leaving him home alone, but repeat the mantra "dogs never destroy out of spite." That fact that he may look guilty when you come home usually stems from past experiences with your irrational home-coming behavior. Here he is finally reunited with his loved one and you start acting crazy. Finally he learns that he'd best act submissive when his crazy owner comes home, especially if the house just happens to be in a shambles.

If you're still not convinced, set up a video camera and watch him while you're gone. You won't see a dog gleefully venting his anger on your home. You'll see a dog pacing, panting, drooling, whining and howling, a dog so upset that he finally has to urinate and defecate with little self-control. Panicked, he tries to bite or dig his way out of the house, centering his attention on areas near doors and windows. Frustrated, he may bark or howl incessantly, quieting only to chew determinedly on your furniture and woodwork. If he's in a crate, he may howl, dig, rip his bedding, bite at the wire, drool, urinate, and defecate. He's not a dog that needs to be punished; he's a dog that needs to be helped.

The number one priority in helping your dog with separation anxiety is to do whatever you can to decrease his anxiety. You'll need to alter many of your behaviors.

Downplay departures. No more long good-byes, or for that matter any cues that you're getting ready to leave. Don't wait until you're ready to leave to turn off the radio or television. By the same token, if you only turn it on when you leave, your dog may already associate its sound with being left alone, so be sure you're not giving your dog that cue anymore. If you use an alarm clock during the week, either find another way to wake up or use it also on weekends. Don't rattle car keys, or make an issue of putting on shoes. This doesn't mean you have to sneak out the door—just don't make a big deal out of it.

Use a safety cue. Just as your dog may have learned to associate some of your unintentional departure cues with your absence, you need to give him some safety cues that he will come to associate with your imminent return. You can spray some air freshener in the room, turn on a radio (if you don't usually have one on), or put down a special bed. These will be used along with a program of graduated departures.

Graduate departures. Leave for only short periods at first— maybe thirty seconds at first. Your goal is to return before your dog has a chance to get upset. Work up to longer times gradually, repeating each level several times before moving to a longer period of absence. Remember, you want him to associate the safety cue with feeling calm. If you must be gone longer than your dog can tolerate, don't give him the safety cue.

Downplay returns. Nobody but a dog can greet your return after a ten-minute absence like you've just been on a trip around the world. But for now, keep the reunion low key. Ignore your dog until he is calm, or better, give him a cue to sit or do some other behavior involving self-control, and then reward him for that.

Consider antianxiety aids. Many dogs may not be calm enough in your absence to make much progress. They may be helped by giving them antianxiety or antidepressant drugs. These drugs must usually be given on a continuous basis, not just when you are going to leave your dog alone. Some drugs for the treatment of panic may be added when the dog is going to be left alone. As with all drug therapy, this is not something you decide to do on your own, but rather should be undertaken under the guidance of a clinical behaviorist.

Canine companions. It seems intuitive that adding a canine companion might provide enough company to calm a dog when left alone, but the company of dogs doesn't satisfy most separation anxiety sufferers. Only when the other dogs provide appropriate social interaction, perhaps in a leadership mode, do they tend to prevent rather than cure separation anxiety. Most separation anxiety is focused on the presence or absence of people, not dogs. This may be because for the older puppy or adult dog, a person is the primary caretaker and essentially takes the place of a parent.

Other Causes of Damage

Not all home destruction in your absence stems from separation distress.

- Destructive behavior can arise from boredom, especially in young dogs. In such cases, however, your dog doesn't usually drool or give other evidence of fearful or escape-oriented behavior.

- In some dogs, destructive behavior can result from outside stimulation, such as cats on the windowsill or neighborhood children teasing the dog. In these cases the dog usually has no signs of fearful or escape behavior but may center its frustration around a particular window.

- Some destructive digging may occur because of pain or because of hormonally induced nesting behavior.

- Some destructive behavior can arise from phobias, such as thunderstorm or gunshot phobias, to stimuli that occur while you happen to be gone. These can be very difficult to differentiate from pure separation distress.

Obsessive-Compulsive Disorders

Like humans, dogs can suffer from a variety of obsessive-compulsive disorders (OCDs). The most common canine examples are tail chasing, flank sucking, imaginary fly biting, and limb licking. Masturbation, eating foreign objects, and eating their own feces may in some cases also rise to the level of OCD. The cause appears to be neurochemical in humans, and presumably also in dogs. Dogs of any breeds can have OCD behaviors. Some breeds tend to be more likely to exhibit certain types of OCD, however. Dobermans are most likely to be flank suckers, Dobermans and Labradors are more likely to be limb lickers, and Bull Terriers tend to compulsively chase, look for, or stare at spots (such as those from laser light toys). These behaviors can become so consuming that dogs do them instead of interacting with their owners or even eating.

Noticing such tendencies and removing the eliciting stimuli from their surroundings may help nip them in the bud. Punishment may cause the dog to stop doing the behavior around the owner, but the dog will usually start back up again once the owner is out of sight. Restraint may similarly prevent the dog from partaking in the activity, and may be necessary in cases resulting in self-mutilation, but restraint won't help the dog get over the compulsion. In fact, it may make the compulsion stronger.

Other causes. Dogs may exhibit some behaviors similar to OCD but which can be attributed to boredom. However, if the dog continues the behavior even when placed in a stimulating environment, or if he foregoes activities that should be more rewarding, such as interacting or eating, then the problem is probably OCD and not boredom. Licking of the body, especially wrists, to the point of hair loss and thickened skin (a condition called acral lick dermatitis) is often a type of OCD, but can sometimes be caused by painful, arthritic joints or by itching. Several infectious, metabolic, or neurological disorders can also cause repetitive and stereotypic behavior such as that seen in OCD. This is why a thorough medical examination should be part of any evaluation of a dog with suspected OCD.

Treatment. Stress appears to be a major component of OCD, so removing as many stressors from your dog's life as possible is step one. The dog should be rewarded for doing some alternative behavior to its compulsive behavior, and especially rewarded for relaxing under circumstances that would normally elicit the compulsive behavior. Concurrent drug therapy under the supervision of a clinical behaviorist will greatly facilitate improvement in most cases of true OCD.

It's not the size of the dog in the fight, it's the size of the fight in the dog."
—Mark Twain (1835–1910)

Chapter 12
Nip It!

Congratulations! You plan to nip aggressive behavior in the bud!

As with people, some degree of aggressive behavior is natural and adaptive. However, aggressive behavior that is dangerous or out of context is unacceptable. Even small dogs have the ability to inflict significant injuries, and their own lives are at risk if they bite people. Do not make excuses for aggressive behavior.

There is no better time to seek the help of a veterinary clinical behaviorist than at the first signs of aggressive behavior in your dog. If your child were acting in ways that could endanger lives, wouldn't you seek professional help? Why, then, do dog owners try to cope with potentially life-threatening behavior without professional help? If you don't cope with aggressive behavior, either you or somebody else could be seriously hurt, or you will wait until it's too late and euthanasia appears to be the only answer.

Aggression problems are more likely to be inborn rather than learned. As hard as you may try, you cannot get a naturally nonaggressive dog to behave aggressively. You can modify the behavior of a naturally aggressive dog, however, either reducing or increasing it.

Types of Aggression

Dog aggression is not a single entity. Clinical behaviorists have categorized canine aggression into various types, some of which will be discussed here. Identifying the type of aggression can rely on subtle cues and astute observation; proper identification is needed before choosing a course of treatment. Some of the major categories include:

- Playful aggression: inappropriately rough play that may get carried away, resulting in actual growls and nips

- Pain aggression: response to pain or the threat of pain, often by grabbing a hand; may be responsible for some cases of biting rough children

- Fear aggression: response to threat of attack, pain, inappropriate punishment, or inappropriately perceived threat. The dog may bark, snarl, tremble, cower, and retreat. Bites are especially likely if the dog is cornered, but may also occur from behind

- Redirected aggression: aggression toward somebody who was not part of the original interactions, such as purposefully biting a person who intervenes in a dog fight

- Interdog aggression: usually occurs within same-sex pairs in socially mature dogs

- Predatory aggression: silent stalking and chasing of animals and sometimes small humans, especially those who squeal, flee, and act unpredictably

- Territorial aggression: protection of yard, car, house, or kennel, or especially any property in which boundaries are clearly defined, such as with a fence

- Protective aggression: protection of one or more family members by standing between, barking, growling, and biting when another person approaches or makes quick movements

- Maternal aggression: hormonally controlled protection of puppies, toys, or nest when nursing or in pseudopregnancy

- Possessive aggression: trying to obtain or refusing to relinquish toys or stolen household objects, growling and possibly biting if somebody attempts to take them

- Food-related aggression: protecting food, treats, and bones from people and other dogs, growling or biting at perceived threats to possession of the food

- Dominance aggression: controlling, threatening, or biting people who the dog perceives to challenge or attempt to control him

- Idiopathic aggression: full aggressive display that appears to occur suddenly out of context

Some of the more common types of aggressive behavior will be discussed in the following pages. In all cases, the information given here for treatment is not meant as a substitute for the diagnosis and advice of a clinical behaviorist who can see your dog in the flesh.

Aggression Myths

- "Dogs that act aggressively are misbehaving." *Not true.* Most aggressive dogs are acting in what they perceive to be an appropriate way. However, because these dogs are not normal, they do not perceive appropriate situations and behaviors normally.

- "A dog with a wagging tail will not bite." *Not true.* A wagging tail indicates only a pleasurable state and a willingness to interact, and biting is a type of interaction and may be pleasurable (at least to the biter).

- "Scruff shakes are good corrections because they mimic the way a mother dog corrects her puppies." *Not true.* In fact, mother dogs rarely, if ever, correct their pups by scruff shaking, nor do other dogs commonly correct each other that way. Scruff shaking can lead to neck injuries and is not suggested as a correction measure.

- "Alpha rolls are good corrections because they mimic the way a dominant dog exerts its dominance over a subordinate dog." *Not true.* In fact, dominant dogs exert most of their dominance simply by ignoring subordinates, much as a celebrity might ignore the masses. Alpha rolls conducted by humans in attempts to subdue an already challenging dog often result in dog bites.

Fear-Related Aggression

Most fearful dogs will either freeze or flee when confronted with something that scares them. Frozen in fear or backed in a corner with no escape, the dog may bite in what he perceives to be self-defense. This is especially true if he's afraid of a person and the person reaches for him. His threat or bite usually makes the person back down, and now the dog has learned a coping tool for the next time he's afraid—and he may not wait until he's cornered to use it.

The language of fear. The fear biter can be distinguished from other biters because his body language screams fear. He tends to crouch, with tail tucked and ears back, perhaps alternately snarling and whimpering, or even snapping in the air. Bites are usually quick and attacks are not sustained. Not every fearful dog lashes out in self-defense. In fact, most shy dogs do not. Most normal dogs remain quiet when frightened.

Treatment guidelines. Therapy should center around helping the dog overcome his fears (see Chapter 11) and better cope with adverse situations. He needs to learn that biting doesn't scare people away, but that doing some tricks or sitting on cue does merit a reward, and possibly at least a temporary reprieve from whoever was bugging him. Meanwhile, take the following precautions:

- Do not place a fear-aggressive dog in situations that could cause him to be afraid.

- Do not punish a fear-aggressive dog for his behavior. Punishment only makes things worse because it verifies his worst fears. In fact, harsh punishment and abuse may be a precipitating factor in fear aggression.

- Do not force a fear-aggressive dog to face his fears, and do not corner or reach for him. These situations greatly increase the chance that he may bite, which in turn becomes self-perpetuating. Instead, call the dog to you and have him act calm or do a trick for a reward.

- Do not reassure or pet a fear aggressive dog while he is acting inappropriately. This gives the dog the message that he is acting appropriately, which he is not.

There's a difference between a frightened dog that will do what it can to avoid a person and then snap when cornered and one that launches a full-fledged attack with imaginary provocation. Although both are potentially dangerous, the latter may be so dangerous that treatment is not a realistic option. In either case, the opinion of a clinical behaviorist is vital.

Territorial Aggression

One of the earliest functions of domesticated dogs was as watchdogs. Many people still keep dogs as watchdogs, but many more dogs are self-appointed watchdogs that often can't discriminate friend from foe. They may bark and bluff because they fear an intruder on their territory, but they do not behave aggressively when away from their territory. Their territory may include their yard, house, car, crate, bed, tie-out area, or a mobile area around the dog or owner. A territory that is clearly marked increases the chances of territorial aggression. Their aggression may be directed toward people or dogs. Normally dogs may bark when their territory is approached by a stranger, but then quiet when the owner tells them to stop. Some dogs, however, cannot be quieted, and may prevent welcome visitors from entering the premises.

Learning. Some components of territorial aggression are learned. The classic example is the mailman who trespasses into the yard, sometimes right up to the front door, on a daily basis. The dog barks and challenges, and sure enough, the intruder turns around and leaves (after he delivers the mail!). As this scenario repeats every day, the dog gains confidence, because in his eyes he is scaring off the intruder time after time. The same may be true of dogs that chase cars driving by on "their" street. The dog gives chase and the car turns tail. Mission accomplished! Eventually these dogs learn to be proactive, challenging all passersby.

The situation is often encouraged by owners who try to calm their dog by reassuring him or distracting him with a game or treat—in both cases rewarding the dog for aggressive behavior. Other owners scream at their dogs, but all that registers with the dog is that Mom is really excited, too—better bark more. Some owners are proud that their dog is such a protector, but an indiscriminate protector is a lawsuit looming.

Treatment. Treat territorial aggression by removing the possibility that your dog will encounter somebody against whom to protect his territory. That means removing him from the fenced yard when passersby are expected, from the front door area when company is expected, and from view of the mailbox when the mailman is expected. Placing a buffer area to separate dogs on opposite sides of a fence may decrease fence fighting when the aggression is aimed at other dogs. The dog should be rewarded for sitting and staying when strangers arrive, and gradually moved closer to them. You can eventually have visitors bring the dog good things. You may need to have them meet initially on neutral territory, with the stranger walking alongside of you while you have the dog attend to you and do some training exercises for rewards. Eventually have your dog sit and then have the stranger offer him a delicious treat. Then you can invite visitors to come into your yard and, gradually, house. You will need to keep your dog on-lead for these exercises. Use of a head halter will give you better and more immediate control of your dog.

Interdog Aggression

Just as with kids, fighting is common among dogs. Unlike the case with kids, serious injuries are not uncommon. In general, males tend to fight with males and females with females. Males seldom attack females, but females sometimes attack males. Castration of males markedly decreases the incidence of fighting, especially among housemates.

Aggression toward strange dogs. Some cases of interdog aggression toward strange dogs may be territorial aggression; in these cases the dogs do not usually threaten and posture as they do before a real dog fight. True aggression toward strange dogs can result from lack of early socialization, bad experiences with other dogs in early life, inadvertent rewards for aggression, or inborn breed predispositions. Gradual conditioning in which the dog is rewarded for behaving nicely and attending to his owner while being exposed to strange dogs can be beneficial. Group obedience classes can be helpful for such training. Because a root problem of many such aggressive dogs is anxiety over the uncertainty of how to relate to strange dogs, drug therapy can sometimes help. Some dogs, however, simply cannot be trusted around strange dogs, and you must make plans to ensure such a dog has outings that don't endanger other dogs. He should be walked only on-leash around strange dogs; a head halter will give you extra control.

Aggression toward housemates. Fighting among housemates is an especially trying situation. It's perfectly natural for housemates to play-fight, and sometimes they can appear quite fierce. But play-fighting dogs usually intersperse lots of freeze-frame play bows in the midst of their play, which lets the other dog know it's all in good fun. Occasionally play fights will get out of hand and escalate into a real scuffle. Real fights can also occur over food or other resources, or when the dogs are otherwise aroused and accidentally hit each other. Usually such fights are more show than real, and they don't last long. Occasionally, however, fights are brutal and even deadly.

In case of a fight. If you see a fight getting ready to start, your natural inclination will be to run toward the combatants-to-be, yelling for them to stop. Chances are they will start before you reach them. That's partially because they interpret your yelling to be encouragement, and partly because you, as the top resource, are often what they are fighting about. Some dogs seem to want to make sure you get to see them, just as fighting boys want to make sure the pretty girl sees them scuffle in the schoolyard. If you can, instead try to distract them with the promise of a walk or toy before the fight breaks out. Although this is bad training in the long run because it rewards aggressive behavior, at least make them then work for their reward by doing some tricks or sitting nicely. If a fight breaks out, you can throw water on them, distract them with clanging pots, try to separate them on opposite sides of a door or with a broom, or throw a blanket over one of them. Just don't do what you are naturally inclined to do, which is stick your arms and legs between them. They won't try to bite you, but they probably will get you by accident.

Physically punishing the dogs for fighting only increases their arousal, and in turn increases the chance of the fight restarting or the aggression being redirected to another dog or to you.

What about just letting them fight? In some cases one fight may put an end to dominance disputes. For that reason many people advocate letting the dogs settle the matter without human intervention. This may be acceptable in some situations, but in cases of intense fighting you're probably going to be paying some steep veterinary bills.

Who's the boss? In a household relationship in which one dog is clearly dominant and the other subordinate, both dogs function within defined boundaries of behavior. The subordinate makes sure the leader knows he is ready to follow. In some cases, though, a younger dog reaches social maturity and may challenge the older dog. The challenges may take the form of a full fight, or they may be subtle, such as blocking access to a door or bowl, stealing the other dog's possessions, pushing the other dog out of preferred sleeping places, or standing over the other dog.

The current leader, sensing these threats (or in some cases erroneously perceiving a younger dog may be challenging), may do a preemptive strike, attacking the younger dog before he tries something.

In most cases, one dog will back down or give up, and the winner will slack off. In some cases, however, the aggressive dog is acting abnormally and does not stop the attack as he should when the other dog cries "Uncle!" Abnormal dogs may never be able to coexist safely with other dogs, at least other dogs they do not like. Many people have learned to carefully divide their houses and time so enemies never get together.

Some dogs are more equal than others. Unfortunately, dog owners love the idea of equality. They treat both dogs the same, something that isn't really right from the leader's point of view. The leader finally jumps the usurper to put him in his place. The owner runs to the defense of the poor abused underdog, coddling him while chastising the aggressor. Since the owner is prime resource number one, the leader is now confused. He should be the one reaping the rewards of his owner's attention. He will have to try harder next time. The subordinate is also confused. Maybe he won after all. He'll have to keep on doing what he was doing. So now the subordinate is primed to transgress on the leader, and the leader primed to attack him for it. Eventually the situation becomes so bad the dogs must be separated, where their dislike of one another grows.

Instead, you should choose the dog that appears to be the leader or eventual leader. He gets the first and best of everything in order to reinforce his higher ranking and bring the dispute to an end. Feed him first, pet him first, and let him have the prime spots over the other dog. You can make up for it to some extent with the other dog when the top dog is out of the room. It may not seem fair by people standards, but it is fair by dog standards. Both your dogs will thank you for it.

A home of his own. Unfortunately, this is not the answer for all cases. Sometimes, one dog is just a bully who will only be satisfied if the other dog is gone. If you reinforce the bully, you reinforce these feelings of entitlement and may make the situation worse. Sometimes two dogs simply cannot coexist, and the kindest and safest solution is to find a single-dog home for one of them.

Predatory Behavior

Dogs are by nature predators, some more than others. Just as some people live to hunt, so do some dogs. Dogs hunt by sniffing out, digging out, running after, and bringing down prey. It's the running after and bringing down that causes the most problems around the neighborhood.

If your dog catches a butterfly, it's considered cute. If he catches a mouse, it's considered handy. If he catches the neighbor's cat, it's considered vicious. The fact that he is being self-sufficient is no consolation to the grieving cat owner. Nor is it an excuse for the dog that runs down a kid on a bicycle, or the pack of dogs that overtakes a running, screaming child.

Hunting versus fighting. Just because a dog chases or even kills another animal, it doesn't mean he is mean. Hollywood movies tend to add sound effects that have dogs or wolves growling and snarling as they bring down their quarry, but hunting dogs don't make these aggression-related noises. Hunting an animal is a distinctly different behavior than fighting an animal, and is usually done silently. It's the difference between a guy having a barroom brawl and one hunting a wild animal; he may sling threats at his fighting opponent, but he won't be trying to frighten off his prey with threats. This is an important distinction when trying to find out what caused an attack. For example, some dogs will run down small dogs and grab them. Those that do so silently probably mistook or viewed the small dog as prey, while those that do so noisily may have been acting out of territorial aggression.

Prevention. Dogs are far less likely to hunt an animal they know. That means that if you plan to keep your cat safe from your dog by never letting the two see one another, you had best be very careful for their entire lives. A better plan is to introduce the two carefully, making sure that the cat can retreat to safety without running. Feed the dog while letting him see you pet and feed the cat, and let the dog know this is a member of the family. That doesn't mean you take dumb chances. When you leave the house you should separate them. It's important that you don't allow the cat in the open where he may take off running, enticing the dog to chase. Most dogs that live with cats are very good with their own cats, but may still chase strange cats. Raising a dog with a variety of cats is probably the best way to make him cat-proof. The same is true whether talking about rabbits, birds, and even kids on bikes. Reward the dog for paying attention to you when one of these potential chasees goes by. Start with slow-speed enticers and gradually work up to faster ones. Of course, your dog shouldn't be running loose on the street whether he chases neighborhood kids or cats or not, but it doesn't hurt to be prepared in case he ever gets out.

Human targets. Infants and toddlers share many characteristics with prey or wounded animals. They have sudden, high-pitched shrieks, they move in an uncoordinated fashion, and they often run unexpectedly. No dog, least of all one with any hint of predatory aggressive tendencies, should be left alone with an infant or toddler.

Food–Related Aggression

Dogs have a natural tendency to protect their food. As puppies, contests over food often establish the first social rankings. But that doesn't make it acceptable behavior in adult dogs.

It's mine! Although food-related aggression can be an early sign of dominance-related problems to come, in most dogs further problems never develop. In dogs, possession is nine-tenths of the law, and a subordinate is within his rights to protect anything within a foot or so of him from his superiors. So don't be so quick to accuse your dog of insubordination just because he doesn't want to give up his chewie to you. It's natural behavior. That doesn't make it tolerable behavior. A dog protecting his food can bite just as hard as one protecting his status.

Bad practices. Often owners create a perfect war that never had to happen because of some idea they have that they will train their dog to allow food to be taken away by repeatedly taking the dog's food away. What does this accomplish? The dog comes to dread the jerk who keeps interrupting his meal, and finally growls to tell him what he thinks of it. The owner says "Aha! I knew he was a biter!" and now punishes the dog. The dog, already irritated, may take the next step and bite. The owner decides the dog can't be trusted and may punish him more until the dog finally subdues, but doesn't forget. He allows the owner to continue with his irritating tests and doesn't protest, until one day a visiting child reaches innocently for his bowl, and the dog lashes out at this new food stealer. Now he is labeled as vicious and taken to the pound. All because his stupid owner had to make a pointless point.

Helping hands. A better scheme is to convince the dog that hands near his food are bringers, not takers. As he is eating, drop special treats into his bowl. If you must take his bowl away, wait until the bowl is empty and then replace it immediately filled with better treats. Convince him that you never take away anything unless you replace it with something better, and he'll soon be begging for you to come near his food bowl. You can also feed him his meals one kibble at a time, dropping each into his bowl as he finishes the one before.

Food-related aggression and other dogs. Dogs that are aggressive to other dogs that come near their food should simply be fed away from other dogs. They should be given chewies and bones only in a private room or in their crate. Never allow a treat to be abandoned in the house somewhere to cause a later dispute, perhaps when you are gone.

Dominance–Related Aggression

Much has been made of the wolf pack hierarchy and its influence on dog behavior in the so-called pack of your family. The idea is that a status-seeking dog, lacking a proper leader, takes over the role and attempts to dominate his people. That's an oversimplification.

More often, a dog doesn't really take over or even try to take over as leader. Instead, he tends to try to control certain situations. The situations may be very selective. A dog may act to resist being bothered or uprooted when resting. He may act in protest to being touched, held, or moved. He may act in response to what he considers challenges, such as eye contact, petting him on the head or back, or bending, reaching, or stepping over him. Such dogs may be fairly amiable in other situations, and even in these particular situations initially.

At least two types of dominance-related aggression are believed to exist. In one type, the dog considers himself in control; in the other, the dog is unsure of his position and uses aggressive behavior as a probe. In either case, the condition usually emerges around the time of social maturity. Neutering can help reduce aggressive behavior, but is seldom as effective once the dog has learned that being aggressive is rewarding.

First signs. Dogs that are predisposed to act in a dominant-aggressive manner may begin with innocuous behaviors. They may demand petting, may repeatedly lean on the owner, or act generally pushy. Most owners don't even notice these behaviors, or if they do, are flattered that the dog is so attentive. They tend to do what the dog wants, and in fact in most dogs this presents no problem. But in some, the dog interprets the owner's behavior as deferring to the dog's demands, and the dog is rewarded for acting assertively. The dog asserts himself more, perhaps pushing his way onto the couch and then grumbling or refusing to move when the owner tries to push him off. Again, many dogs that resist and grumble are just fine. But some progress to growling and biting.

Punishment pitfalls. Once the dog begins to act overtly aggressive, the owner may try to punish him. Punishing causes the dominant-aggressive dog to escalate his aggression, however. The owner is placed in a power struggle in which punishment and aggressive behavior feed on each other until the dog is subdued or, more often, the owner retreats out of fear for herself or of hurting the dog. The dog chalks up a victory.

Now the dog has been rewarded for acting aggressively, and everything associated with that rewarding event is part of a learned scenario that will more likely bring on another such outburst. The dog has also gained more confidence from being able to control his environment and owner. If his owner tries to punish him, the resulting pain or anger can escalate the dog's aggression, sending him into a rage. Usually the owner, fearful now, backs off. The dog has won again. The dog has also learned that he needs to watch out for his owner, and may start behaving aggressively to preempt any challenges by his owner. It becomes a vicious cycle of growing aggression. A dog at this level needs professional help. It is seldom safe or effective to try to treat such a dog on your own. Get immediate professional help from a certified clinical behaviorist.

Bad advice. Typical advice for an owner with a dog suspected of acting as an alpha, or dominant, dog is for the owner to instead dominate the dog, often with alpha-rolls or neck shakes, supposedly in imitation of a wolf pack leader. In fact, wolf pack leaders seldom resort to threats or violence. They tend to be benevolent leaders. They do not abuse their power by threatening, bothering, or stealing from subordinates. They control the pack by initiating and leading activities and by becoming the center of attention. Rather than using force, wolf leaders tend to rely on being somewhat aloof, which tends to bring out displays of affection from subordinates. Affection not only increases the likelihood of group cohesion, but also decreases the likelihood of aggression. In a cooperative pack, maintaining social order through bonding is a better choice than doing so through coercion. This is not to say that fights never erupt. When two wolves are near equals in status, the more dominant of the two is more likely to issue threats toward the other, and the more submissive is more likely to issue challenges. In either case a fight may break out.

Treatment. This suggests that if you want to establish yourself as leader, you're better off to do so not with constant exhibitions of domination, but by being a clear and effective leader. Avoid situations that elicit aggressive behavior. If the dog protests when you try to get him off the sofa, make it so he can't get up there in the first place. If he doesn't tolerate being reached for, don't reach for him. Do not try to bring on a confrontation.

Establish your position by remaining somewhat aloof and not allowing the dog to take liberties with you such as pulling you around or jumping on you. Be a leader by leading the dog in cooperative activities such as walks and training games. This is not unlike how a good parent acts. You wouldn't take every opportunity to dominate a child. That's just being a bully. Instead you earn respect by being clear in what's expected, guiding the child through various experiences, rewarding the child for cooperation, and letting the child know when her behavior is disrespectful or out of bounds.

Tough love. A dominant-aggressive dog needs tough love. That means you can't fawn on him, even though you love him. Fawning is what subordinates do to their leader. You want your dog to fawn on you, and one way that might help bring him around is to ignore him for several days. He may demand your attention, pushing his head under your hand for petting, poking you with his nose, or placing his foot in your lap, but that's not good enough. Leader dogs grant their attention only when they feel like it, not at the beck and call of subordinates. Of course, it hurts too much to ignore him completely or forever, so have him earn your attention by sitting nicely when you ask him to. Make him earn it. In fact, make him earn everything. Meals, treats, games, even walking through doorways should be dependent on his sitting on cue for just a second beforehand. Reward him for calm, happy behavior, especially when he is doing something you ask of him. Nothing in life is free, but it doesn't have to cost a fortune.

It's often said that children want rules. Nowhere is the analogy as clear as with dominant-aggressive dogs. They need to know where they fit in the social system, and they need for it to be absolutely clear. This doesn't mean you need to be violent, simply consistent.

"A dog's bark may be worse than his bite, but it's never quite so personal."
—**Unknown**

Congratulations!

You're on your way to being the perfect puppy parent! Now quit reading and go spend time with your dog!

Resources

For more information on:

Evolution and Domestication
Coppinger, Raymond and Lorna. *Dogs: A Startling New Understanding of Canine Origin, Behavior, and Evolution.* New York: Scribner, 2001.

Serpell, James (Editor). *The Domestic Dog: Its Evolution, Behaviour, and Interactions with People.* New York: Cambridge University Press, 1995.

Genetics and Behavior
Scott, John Paul, and Fuller, John L. *Genetics and the Social Behavior of Dogs.* Chicago: University of Chicago Press, 1965.

Stockard, Charles. *The Genetic and Endocrine Basis for Differences in Form and Behavior.* Philadelphia: Wistar Institute, 1941.

Choosing a Dog
Coile, D. Caroline. *Encyclopedia of Dog Breeds* (2nd edition). Hauppauge, NY: Barron's Educational Series, 2005.

Training and Learning
Alexander, Melissa. *Click for Joy!* Waltham, MA: Sunshine Books, 2003.

Burch, Mary R. and Bailey, Jon S. *How Dogs Learn.* New York: Howell Book House, 1999.

Lindsey, Steven R. *Handbook of Applied Dog Behavior and Training. Vol 1: Adaptation and Learning.* Ames, IA: Iowa State Press, 2000.

Reid, Pamela. *Excel-erated Learning.* Berkeley, CA: James and Kenneth Publishers, 1996.

Taunton, Stephanie J., and Smith, Cheryl S. *The Trick Is in the Training.* Hauppauge, NY: Barron's Educational Series, Inc., 1998.

Tillman, Peggy. *Clicking with Your Dog.* Waltham, MA: Sunshine Books, 2000.

Behavior Problems
Askew, Henry R. *Treatment of Behavior Problems in Dogs and Cats: A Guide for the Small Animal Veterinarian* (2nd edition). Oxford: Blackwell Science, 2003.

Lindsey, Steven R. *Handbook of Applied Dog Behavior and Training. Vol. 2: Etiology and Assessment of Behavior Problems.* Ames, IA: Iowa State Press, 2001.

Overall, Karen. *Clinical Behavioral Medicine for Small Animals.* St Louis, MO: Mosby, 1997.

Bonding Activities
Coile, D. Caroline. *Beyond Fetch: Fun, Interactive Activities for You and Your Dog.* New York: Wiley, 2003.

Coile, D. Caroline. *How Smart Is Your Dog? 30 Fun Science Activities with Your Pet.* New York: Sterling, 2003.

Organizations
American College of Veterinary Behaviorists
Dr. Bonnie Beaver
Department of Small Animal Medicine and Surgery
Texas A&M University
College Station, TX 77843-4474
www.veterinarybehaviorists.org

Animal Behavior Society
Central Office, Indiana University
2611 East 10th Street #170
Bloomington, IN 47408-5541
www.animalbehavior.org

Association of Companion Animal Behavior Counselors
www.animalbehaviorcounselors.org

Association of Pet Dog Trainers (APDT)
150 Executive Center Drive Box 35
Greenville, SC 29615
800-PET-DOGS
www.apdt.com